COLLECTOR'S ENCYCLOPEDIA OF MUNCIE POTTERY

IDENTIFICATION & VALUES

J ON R ANS & M ARK E CKELMAN

COLLECTOR BOOKS

A Division of Schroeder Publishing Co., Inc.

The current values in this book should be used only as a guide. They are not intended to set prices, which vary from one section of the country to another. Auction prices as well as dealer prices vary greatly and are affected by condition as well as demand. Neither the authors nor the publisher assumes responsibility for any losses that might be incurred as a result of consulting this guide.

Searching For A Publisher?

We are always looking for knowledgeable people considered to be experts within their fields. If you feel that there is a real need for a book on your collectible subject and have a large comprehensive collection, contact Collector Books.

On the Cover

Lovebird vase, shape #193, gloss light green, marked 4, $500.00–550.00.
Vase, shape #100 - 12", matte green over rose dripped, marked 2A, $225.00–250.00.
Vase, shape #134 - 10", matte blue over white dripped, marked 2, $175.00–200.00.
Fan vase, shape #186 - 7", blue peachskin, unmarked, $125.00–150.00.
Candlesticks, shape #149 - 6", matte blue over white dripped, marked 2B, $225.00–250.00 pair.
Star vase, shape #312 - 5", blue peachskin, marked A, $300.00–350.00.
Candlestick, shape #152 - 3", matte blue over rose dripped, marked, $125.00–150.00.
Vase, shape 480 - 3½", matte white over blue dripped, marked Muncie - 3A, $70.00–90.00.

Cover design: Beth Summers
Book design: Karen Geary

COLLECTOR BOOKS
P.O. Box 3009
Paducah, KY 42002-3009

CONTENTS

ABOUT THE AUTHORS

Both residents of Muncie, Indiana, Jon Rans and Mark Eckelman independently developed an interest in Muncie Pottery as an art form and as a part of their local community's history long before its recent surge in popularity. Rans, an expert in pottery restoration, started collecting Muncie Pottery in 1984 and began to research the history of the company in earnest in 1994. Due to the destruction of the company's records by fire, gathering information has required countless hours tracking down documents and interviewing former employees and their families. Eckelman started collecting Muncie Pottery and studying its many shapes, glazes, and identifying features in 1988. Since then, he has established himself as a top collector/dealer of Muncie Pottery. Prices and descriptions of glazes, shapes and their relative rarity are based on auction prices and experience. This book is the result of their collaboration.

INTRODUCTION

Underrated and overlooked for many years, Muncie Pottery, produced in Indiana during the 1920s and 1930s, has gained interest from collectors across the country. Its rise in popularity has been partially due to its rarity but also the collector's appreciation of the honest style and harmonious use of colors in the various glazes. With this acceptance into the circle of collectible potteries, prices have seen increases from several dollars to several hundred dollars per piece. As almost all records of the pottery were long ago destroyed in the numerous fires that plagued the company, research has been an exercise in persistence. The role this pottery played in the development of personnel as well as its influence on other art potteries of the day should not be discounted. It was a testing ground for a grand idea, and many dedicated and visionary people were associated with its development.

The story of Muncie Pottery is entwined with its parent company, Gill Clay Pot Company, its creators, and the period between the two World Wars that created the climate for its inceptions and the conditions for its demise.

In our search for information and goods from these companies, we have been fortunate enough to meet many wonderful people. Inspiration, encouragement, and information were forthcoming from former employees, fellow collectors, and others who were doing research on related subjects. We would like to thank the following people for sharing with us: The Aladdin Knights of the Mystic Light, Bracken Library Special Collections (Ball State University) and archivist Nancy Turner, Bill Courter, David Dilly and L & W Books, Dennis Donovan, Jim Dragoo of Dragoo Auction Company, David Gifford, Minnetrista Cultural Center (Muncie, Ind.), Muncie Public Library, Muskingum County Library, and Richard Sacksteder.

We are deeply indebted to the following people who allowed us into their homes and lives and sacrificed time and energy critical in making this book a reality: Pat and Gerald Hahn, Kathleen Scott, Jennifer Evans and Larry Zimpleman of the Zimpleman Art Studio (Kirklin, Ind.), Fred and Karen Diehl, and Fred Wilkins.

Also special thanks are extended to Nicol Knappen, Edward Arnold, and the Wisconsin Pottery Association for their help on the Wis-Art section. Also to Ralph Wright, Mike Borg, and the Boys Town Hall of History for going beyond the call of duty in assisting us with the Boys Town information.

Last, but certainly not least, our wives, Rita Rans and Julie Eckelman, who made this project possible by encouraging us through every step of our collecting, researching, and writing. Without their unwavering support, this effort would never have come to fruition. To them we owe the greatest gratitude.

JAMES S. GILL AND SONS

According to the 1939 *History of Delaware County,* the Gill family had their roots in Bristol, one of England's oldest seaports and a noted center for glass and pottery production. The overcrowding and dismal living conditions brought on by the Industrial Revolution drove men to seek their fortunes elsewhere; James S. Gill was one of these.

Passage by sea was a difficult ordeal in the 1840s when James and Emma chose to start a new life in America. Their destination was Wheeling, West Virginia, where James would pursue his trade as potmaker, a specialized trade in high demand by the area's developing glass manufacturers.

Gill made clay pots, the large clay vessels used to hold the raw ingredients of glass during the intense heat of their stay inside the furnaces. The extreme temperatures that were required for this remarkable transformation demanded the clay pots be made carefully in order to avoid disaster. Various clays had to be selected, ground, blended, aged, then built up by hand to form these huge vessels, some of which weighed more than a ton. After a slow air drying period, they were placed in the kiln for firing. It was the practice then for most of these "hand glass" companies to make their own pots, hiring potmakers to produce the clay pots on site.

After working for years in many of Wheeling's glass factories, James decided to go into the clay pot business. In 1882, James and Emma moved their growing family, daughter Hannah and four sons, Charles J., Harry R., William H, and Frank O., across the Ohio River to Bellaire, Ohio, and created James S. Gill and Sons. This company specialized in refractory clay products for the region's growing glass industry for the next decade.

Engraved Gill letterhead from 1892.

GILL BROTHERS

In 1892 after the death of James Gill, a decision was made to move the corporate offices of the firm to Muncie, Indiana, while maintaining the Bellaire plant. The expansion was to take advantage of the unprecedented business opportunities generated by the recently discovered Trenton gas field. The field, found in 1886 near Eaton, Indiana, was at the time the largest known in the world. The Gill brothers were among many businessmen attracted to the area by Muncie's Citizens Enterprise Company, publicly held promotional organization whose goal was to aggressively market Muncie to prospective industry. Gas wells with colorful names like Jumbo and Major were big attractions, and monthly train excursions brought interested parties from as far away as Buffalo, New York. As a promotion, what was believed to be an inexhaustible supply of gas was ignited at the well heads. The burning wells were a beacon that attracted speculators and entrepreneurs looking for cheap and abundant fuel.

Before the discovery of the Trenton Field, there were only four glass firms in Indiana; after 1886, dozens opened in east central Indiana. These were ready customers for Gill products. The corporate name was changed to Gill Brothers and Plant #1 was built in Muncie at Woods Avenue and Blaine Street, now 14th and Penn streets.

In 1895, Gill Brothers had 40 employees and a monthly payroll of $2,000.00 as stated in the 1939 *History of Delaware County*, including James Gill's grandson, 18-year-old Charles O. Grafton who worked as a "roll boy" delivering properly prepared rolls of clay to the potters. With six up-draft coal-fired kilns, the Gill Brothers plant was adjacent to one of its best customers, the Ball Brothers Canning Jar factory, one of six glass manufacturers in Muncie. From Plant #1, tank block was produced and shipped by rail to customers across the United States and Canada.

By 1900, there were 110 glass companies in Indiana, and most were in the Muncie area. A panic developed when the gas fields began in fail in 1901; they were mostly depleted by 1910. Ball Brothers, Hemingray insulators, and several other major glass producers remained in business, providing Gill with a local market. Around 1900, an accident at the plant resulted in serious injury to Frank and William Gill. On January 13, 1903, William Gill died. Charles Grafton was promoted to factory manager in 1904. Frank Gill remained active in the firm until 1913 when he took a position with Bersback, Maloney & Company, sales agent for manufacturers specializing in crockery, glassware, and lamps. The company was located in Denver, Colorado, and also served Wyoming and New Mexico. By 1921, brother Harry Gill was the company owner and had extended the sales territory to Utah, Montana, and Idaho. He represented Imperial Glass, Brush-McCoy Pottery, and Muncie Pottery among others.

JUMBO

Illustration of Jumbo.

Photo of worker and clay pot from 1916.

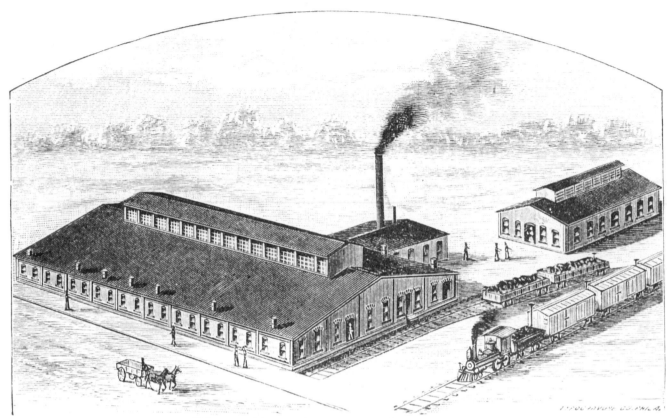

Glass Pot Factory—Gill Bros.'

Engraving of Plant #1.

Gill factory clay pot room.

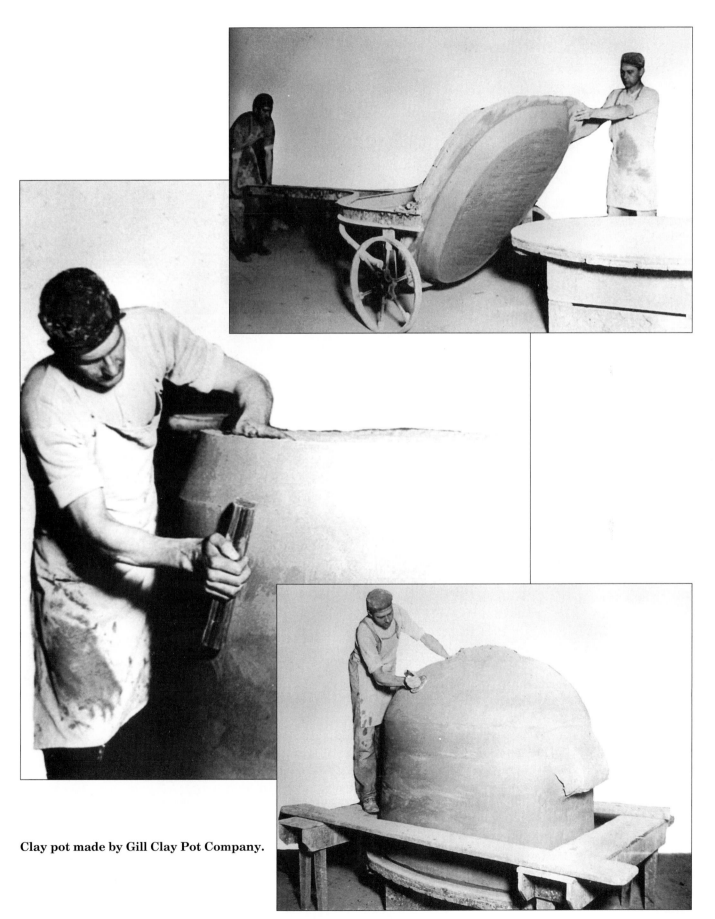

Clay pot made by Gill Clay Pot Company.

Clay pot.

Display of crucibles.

THE GILL CLAY POT COMPANY

The company was reorganized and incorporated as the Gill Clay Pot Company on March 19, 1908, when Charles Grafton, Charles Gill, and Harry Gill bought the interest of William Gill. Charles Gill's son, John H., joined the company in 1910 and became secretary in 1917. Charles Grafton's father-in-law, James Boyce, in 1911 sold the company the Tappan Shoe Manufacturing Company complex, built in the 1890s, which had been empty for several years.

The condition of the property was poor, and modernization of the new Gill Plant #2 took three years. Several additions were made to existing buildings along with oil-fired kilns and a new power plant. Electric motors were added to all the machinery. A new railroad spur was installed on the east side of the plant in 1912, and in 1919 the grounds in front were enhanced by a park area for the enjoyment of the workers.

Tank block, clay pots, crucibles, and later pottery were manufactured from this factory. Tank block was used as a furnace liner by companies making cheap glassware, bottles, fruit jars, and insulators. Crucibles were used for melting and pouring molten material. Clay pots for melting batch glass were sold in greenware or fired and were used by finer glass companies making cut, opal, and colored glass. President Charles Gill did most of the traveling and much of the selling for the firm, leaving Charles Grafton in charge of daily management.

Charles J. Gill, 1935.

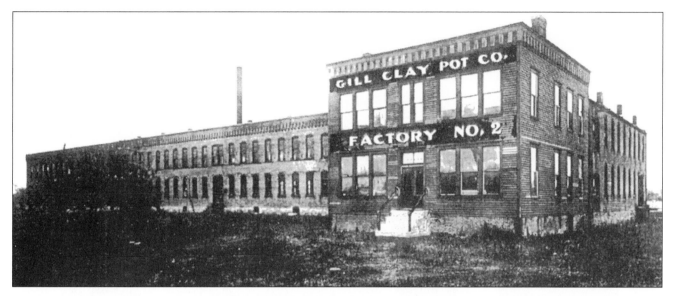

Gill Plant #2, ca. 1918 – 1919.

Charles Gill had grown up in the glass business and was president of Crystal Glass Company of Bridgeport, Ohio, which also operated West Virginia Glass Works in Martins Ferry, Ohio. He was considered an "old glass man," on familiar terms with the management of most American art glass houses. A letter dated Oct. 5, 1911, to Merchants National Bank of Muncie includes a customer list of Gill Clay Pot that reads like a who's who of the American glass industry. Not only utilitarian-ware firms like Ball Brothers and Corning Glass, but also finer art-glass makers like Fostoria, Steuben, Indiana Glass, Phoenix Glass, and Consolidated Lamp and Glass were represented.

In 1914, World War I embroiled Europe, and American business increased because of production demands for the war effort. Due to an embargo, German refractory products and German clays, viewed as the finest quality, became unavailable, and American glass and metal manufacturers were forced to use only domestic products. Gill had used a mixture of Ohio, Missouri, and German clays and was forced to find a substitute for the foreign clay. The problem was addressed in an article in 1920 by Charles Grafton, "The Art of Pot Making," in the *Journal of the American Ceramics Society*:

"There is no single American clay that was a perfect substitute for German clay. But a guarded blend of three American clays, none from Indiana, was not only a substitute but in fact a superior product in many cases."

Advertisement, ca. 1920.

Logo from company letterhead, ca. 1921.

Gill employee at grinding machine.

Sectioning clay at the Pug Mill prior to aging.

Gill Clay Pot Company stock certificate.

THE GERMAN - AMERICAN CLAY COMPANY

Established on July 27, 1915, and located at the same Lincoln Street address as Gill Clay Pot Company, the German-American Clay Company Inc. specialized in mining and shipping high-grade clays. It had a familiar line-up of officers: Charles Gill, president; John Gill, vice president, and Charles Grafton, secretary-treasurer. M.W. Muenster was mine superintendent, and George W. Cochran, secretary-treasurer of Ohio Valley Clay Company was on the board of directors.

Office at North Lincoln Street, ca. 1919.

German clay was purchased from J. Goebel & Company of New York, and an Indiana mine was located in Jasper County. Milling, blending, aging, and shipping took place at the Gill plant. The company name was changed in 1917 to American Clay Company to present a more patriotic image.

Charles Grafton held controlling interest in the new company with 508 shares of stock. He would acquire the shares of George Cochran, J.M. Lawbie, A.S. Gopfi, James Hogan, and E.M. Moody by 1925, leaving Charles and John Gill with one share each. Though not listed in the Muncie City Directory after 1922, this company had a direct impact on the development of refractory and pottery clay formulas and on the creation of Muncie Clay Products, a subsidiary company with Charles Grafton in creative control.

German-American Clay company stock certificate.

The American Clay Company mine owned by the Gill Clay Pot Company located in southern Indiana.

Young workers relax while having their picture taken.

Processing raw clay at the mine.

Clay pits filled with aging clay.

Workers tramping clay to prepare it for the potters.

MUNCIE CLAY PRODUCTS

It was Christmas 1918, and there was a new optimistic outlook in the air. World War I had just ended and business was flourishing. Grafton and Gill decided to utilize their abundant stockpile of high-grade clays and develop a more commercial pottery enterprise. They also added a line of utilitarian wares and art pottery for consumers. The new subsidiary was called Muncie Clay Products and officers were Charles Grafton, president; Charles Gill, vice president; Clealon V. Grafton, treasurer and general manager; and Elza F. Heistand, secretary.

Charles Grafton.

Gill Clay Pot and American Clay had done quite well during the war years. Art pottery production was a logical area of expansion for the companies since it would use much of the same equipment as crucible manufacture. The new venture would make up for the expected decrease in demand for refractory products. The name Muncie Clay Products was chosen on December 27, 1918, and letters of incorporation, with $10,000 listed in capital, were filed on January 9, 1919. Charles Benham, Charles Grafton's son-in-law, also joined the company about this time.

In 1921, the remaining interest of Harry Gill in Gill Clay Pot was purchased by Charles Grafton and Charles Gill. Grafton then became treasurer and general manager of Gill operations. A new building to accommodate the art pottery was built in 1923 on the grounds west of the old factory. It had two updraft gas-fired kilns, one 16-foot and one 12-foot. The new division employed 25 to 30 people, and total Gill employment never exceeded 150.

Crucible production continued at this new division and sales actually increased due to a three-lipped crucible developed and patented by Gill. The new design aided workers by enabling them to pour the molten contents from almost any position, unlike the old style that had only two positions and was cumbersome to handle. Limited art pottery experimentation began in 1920 and 1921. In 1922, early production pieces were made. A mixture of Canadian, Tennessee, English, and Indiana clays was judged as the most suitable for the clay body. Pieces from this period are not marked and have a dense quality. Many were designed and thrown by a German master potter now known only as the "Dutchman." To show off his expertise, he would throw long-stemmed champagne glasses on the wheel. He was held in high regard by fellow employees and remained with the pottery for many years. It is quite possible the letter "K" is his mark.

In 1922, A.E. (Boris) Trifonoff, a designer and master mold maker, was hired to develop the artistic pottery line, including molds and early production glazes. Trifonoff, also a musician and poet, was born in 1882 in Perm, Russia, and had studied ceramics at the Academi Julien in Paris. He worked as designer for the American Encaustic Tile Company of Zanesville, Ohio, from 1918 to 1921. During his short time as ceramist at Muncie Clay Products, he produced a large variety of production molds for many of the well-known Muncie shapes,

The 1918 entry in the Muncie Armistice Parade by Gill Clay Pottery Co. employees. Donations were tossed into the large banners by spectators, raising $186.00 for the Gold Star Mothers.

including pieces with carved animal designs and carved relief plaques. Rainbow-hued basic gloss glazes, similar to the Ohio tile glazes, can be attributed to him. Known as "The Mad Russian," he left the Muncie area in 1923–1924.

In 1926, Trifonoff worked at S.A. Weller Co. of Zanesville, Ohio, and he was hired in the late 1920s by Camark Pottery of Camden, Arkansas. While at Camark, he produced volumes of production molds, some of which are very similar to his Muncie Clay Products designs. Trifonoff also worked at Mt. Clemens Pottery, Mt. Clemens, Michigan, and he retired in 1952 from Homer Laughlin China Co. of East Liverpool, Ohio, where he had been head molder for 8½ years.

A. E. Trifonoff.　　　**James Wilkins.**

In 1923, James Wilkins was hired as foreman of the art pottery department. Wilkins was born in 1870 in Bristol, England, a fourth generation potter. He worked at one of the Bristol potteries as master potter, ceramist, and superintendent. The Wilkins family came to the United States in 1914. Wilkins and his son, William, were associated with the Lewis Institute (now the Illinois Institute of Technology) in Chicago as instructors. James Wilkins worked there from 1919 to 1923, when he became head ceramist for Muncie Clay Products, finishing the designs' molds and glazes for the "Artistic Pottery" line by 1924. He developed a popular new line of matte glazes in 1925. Most of Muncie's more unusual glazes are due to his experimentation.

View of Gill complex, ca. 1930s. Art pottery building shown at the left.

THE MUNCIE POTTERIES

By the early 1930s, the slump that would later be known as the Great Depression was apparent, but few people expected it to continue. During previous financial panics, the downturn had reversed itself in a year or two. The pottery operated on a part-time basis during 1930.

In January 1931, the pottery reopened and reorganized, changing its corporate name to the Muncie Potteries. Charles Grafton was president, Elze F. Heistand, vice president, and Charles Benham, operations manager. According to Benham, quoted in the January 27, 1931 *Muncie Morning Star,* "The new company will continue the manufacture of high quality art pottery which is now being marketed under the trade name Muncie Pottery. The factory has sufficient orders on hand and in prospect to insure continuing operation through the year." The company increased its capital from $10,000 to $100,000.

The clay body also was changed at this time. Southern Indiana clays were removed, and Tennessee ball clay, English ball clay, flint, and feldspar were combined in the new mixture. The resulting clay body appears white, as opposed to the gray and almond coloring of the previous mixtures.

Production continued throughout the Depression, but payment for the finished goods slowed. Lamp production, so important at the beginning, was no longer a prime revenue source. At one point, employees worked for promissory notes, paid when payment was received by the company. During this time, Gill Clay Pot Company began to produce a cast-stone product for the construction trade using tank block clay mix. Developed by employee Pete Elliott, it looked somewhat like quarried limestone.

The Muncie Potteries, along with many of its glass-manufacturing customers, was severely affected by the economic times and would barely survive into the 1930s. The gift shop that operated on the top floor of its offices closed in 1931, and the firm shifted to a wholesale only enterprise. In a desperate effort to save the company, new pottery designs were introduced with many small pieces under five inches. About this time, juice sets in bittersweet glazes were produced, along with new lamp designs. Some of the most striking glazes date to this period.

Muncie Pottery Incorporated, as it was listed in the 1940 Muncie City Directory, ceased production on January 20, 1939, and shut down operations completely on July 8, 1939, after a nine-year loss of $15,000. Charles Grafton, the driving force behind the pottery, died on March 24, 1939. Charles Benham remained with the company, selling what merchandise he could from the office on Lincoln Street until November 30, 1940. In January 1942, the remaining assets of Charles Grafton, stock in the American Clay Company, were transferred to Gill Clay Pot

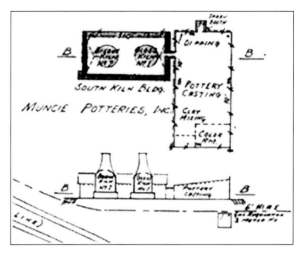

Detail from Indiana inspection report, June 1939.

Muncie Potteries stock certificate, 1931 issue.

Company in settlement of the $15,000 advanced to him by Charles Gill to continue the operation of the pottery in the 1930s. The Muncie Potteries Inc. was liquidated on March 30, 1942. The remaining stock of both glazed and bisque pottery was sold by the bushel basket for $1.00.

The buildings that housed the pottery were used by the Gill Clay Pot Company until an accidental gas explosion destroyed one of the kilns in 1948 or 1949. The remaining section of art pottery building adjacent to the kilns burned in 1951. Gill Clay Pot Company survived as one of three companies manufacturing glass melting pots in the United States until the accidental death of owner John H. Gill in 1966.

After Gill's death, company accountant Robert Hughes bought Gill Clay Pot Corporation from the Gill estate. In the time it had lain vacant, it had become a hang-out for vagrants, animals, and vandals, and all had taken their toll on the old buildings. The remaining Gill Plant #2 caught fire on February 6, 1968, and was destroyed. The property was condemned by city officials, and the damaged buildings leveled that same year. The Lincoln Street site is now just an overgrown lot on the old east end of town. All that remains are pottery shards, pieces of kiln brick, and a stand of trees, some almost 40 years old, growing over the remnant foundations of the old abandoned pottery site — a sad ending to the dreams of its founders and the efforts of its employees.

Fire at the Gill Clay Pot Company, February 6, 1968.

Photos from the 1968 *Muncie Star* showing sheriff inspecting office and kiln conditions.

PRODUCTION

The American Arts and Crafts movement influenced many Muncie pottery designs. Charles Grafton visualized designs based on classic Grecian, Egyptian, and American Indian shapes. These were created with wooden mockups in the mold department by James Wilkins. Production molds were cast from the mockups by Napoleon Noland. Slip casting was done by Willard Wright, with glaze dipping by John Joiner. Kilns were fired to as least cone 10 (2,381° Fahrenheit) turning the stoneware white and vitrifying the pottery in the bisque firing. The kilns required 46 hours of constant monitoring by Barney Barnes to complete one firing cycle. Some of the regular finishing women were Pauline Puterbaugh, Mabel C. Miller, Donna Mercer, and Ethel Bailey Schrecongost, whose Roman numeral I can be seen on pieces throughout the pottery's lifespan.

Hand-thrown shapes were produced by many, now unknown, transient potters who migrated to Muncie from the potteries and clay fields of Ohio, Tennessee, and Kentucky.

The pottery was cast thicker than most pottery of the day, and this accounts for the heavy feel of the pottery and many of the manufacturing problems. Although production was high, the company lost large amounts of pottery through manufacturing problems. First-quality pieces were difficult to obtain, and pieces with minor flaws were considered saleable. Glazes were fired to cone 9 (2,345° Fahrenheit). Some finished pieces remained semi-porous after firing, revealing a defect in both clay body and glaze compounds. The company was unable or unwilling to correct the problems, and some pieces were coated on the inside with beewax as a temporary seal.

Although the factory had been improved, conditions were far from pleasant. Lung disease, caused by large amounts of clay dust in the air, took its toll. Most employees worked on a piece rate. The least of them were the laborers who endlessly tramped the tons of clay with their bare feet, "wedging" the aged slabs in preparation for the potter's wheel.

THE LINES OF MANUFACTURE

Wholesale lamp base production was heavy in the early years of the pottery; a reported 8,000 pieces of one popular design were shipped weekly to satisfy increasing demand as the nation converted to electric light. The sales force represented the wares to retailers throughout the country, and local residents could buy them at the pottery's own retail outlet at the plant. During the 1920s and 1930s, thousands of the bases were sold as both "fitted and unfitted." Catalogs from the period show more than 40 styles, many based on the company's vase designs, in glazes varying from gloss to matte in the same palette used on the art pottery line.

Lamp bases also were manufactured for three Muncie lamp companies, R. Milt Retherford Manufacturing Company, Roland C. Streeter Lamp Company, and Aladdin Manufacturing Company. Aladdin, which made both metal and pottery lamps, was one of the largest clients of the pottery and distributed its products worldwide.

"Rainbow Art Pottery" as advertised by L.S. Ayers was the name given to Muncie pottery because of the color varieties of gloss and matte glazes that were developed by Trifonoff and Wilkins. The line was not expensive ("Fine pottery everyone could afford") and was marketed to dry goods stores, florists, jewelry shops, and department stores. The company also had a fully staffed, wholesale showroom in the Merchandise Mart in Chicago. Some of its best customers included L.S. Ayers and Charles Mayer and Company, both of Indianapolis; Marshall Fields and Company, Chicago; and H.S. Pogue Company of Cincinnati. The wares also were sold in a major center of the American Arts and Crafts movement, East Aurora, New York, home of Elbert Hubbard and The Roycroft Shops. The line eventually included garden pottery, bird baths, wall pockets, paperweights, baskets, bowls, vases, bookends, candlesticks, planters, tea sets, juice and water sets, and little brown jugs.

Many examples of hand-painted bisque (once-fired, unglazed pottery) exist. These were seconds or overstocks that were sold or given to the Boy Scouts and other groups that painted them for gifts or fund raising. Bisque also was sold to schools for glazing and firing by art students.

Ayers advertisement, November 1926.

Consistent similarities appear between Muncie Pottery shapes and glass in the Consolidated Glass catalog, most notably the lines of Martele (1926), Catalonian (1927), Florentine (1927), and Ruba Rombic (1928). These can be attributed to designer Reuben Haley, who was influenced by the landmark 1925 Paris International Exposition of Decorative and Industrial Arts where the acclaimed Rene Lalique had exhibited a variety of his designs. When the exhibit toured the United States in 1926, Lalique glass was well-represented. The lovebird, goldfish, and grasshopper designs of Muncie Pottery are Haley designs and are reminiscent of Lalique's work.

Muncie Scouts exhibit, ca. 1927–1928.

Muncie's Old Spanish line has a hand-thrown look and is similar to pieces in the Catalonian hand-wrought glass catalog. The Florentine line of glassware has an etched motif. Muncie's versions are smooth but use the same basic forms. The Ruba Rombic line has the geometric construction of Art Deco with its severely Cubist forms.

Consolidated Glass introduced its Haley-designed lines in January 1928. There is evidence that Haley's designs for Muncie Pottery also date to 1928. Haley had formed his own design and mold company in 1925, selling molds and licensing his designs on a royalty basis. Not all of Haley's pottery designs were manufactured by Muncie. Many American and European manufacturers copied the popular designs, making identification somewhat difficult.

Mold making: First a model is turned; then a master mold is cast. From this production, molds are cast. After a few weeks of drying, they are stored, ready for use in the casting department.

Slip being poured into molds. Excess slip was drained into center chute after sufficient time allowed the clay to set.

Hand turning at a potter's wheel using a jigger.

Row of workers using jiggers.

Greenware being cleaned and finished before the first firing.

Casters, molders, and finishers, 1927–1928.

MUNCIE GLAZES

Muncie Pottery developed most of its glazes in its early years, and while many people probably played a role, the primary credit rests with two or three individuals. Worker Ray Jones, in an interview with Jon Rans, described the first person working with glazes as "The Dutchman." He said the Dutchman spent his day "sitting in a back area of the building throwing pots and working on other aspects of making pottery." Jones is adamant that the Dutchman was the first person creating pottery at the factory, but unfortunately, no records exist from the period.

The first recorded designer/ceramist with the company was Boris Trifonoff, who arrived around 1922. Much of the early glaze development came during his tenure. Since Muncie was known as the Rainbow Pottery at the time, it can be assumed the majority of glazes he developed were simple colors like black, blue, green, yellow, and white. Trifinoff left in 1923 or 1924.

James Wilkins arrived in 1923 to take over as head ceramist, and it is unknown whether he and Trifinoff ever shared duties. Wilkins accidentally discovered the peachskin glaze early in his work at Muncie. According to old stories, a kiln mistake resulted in a pot acquiring a glaze that one worker remarked "looks like a peach's skin." Wilkins worked to perfect the peachskin, as well as most of Muncie's well-known drip and matte glazes. He perfected many of his glazes by the mid 1920s but developed and introduced a few new ones into the early 1930s. Experimentation in the last years of the company resulted in several strange glazes and shapes occasionally found in the pottery.

The role of Wilkins' son, William, is uncertain. While never an employee of Muncie Pottery, he seemed to have had access to his father's glaze formulas. He used exact copies while employed at Wis-Art and during his long and successful career at Boys Town.

So many companies were producing pottery in the early 1900s it is nearly impossible to prove a particular ceramist developed a specific glaze. However, crediting Muncie Pottery with the refinement and perfection of the many drip and peachskin glazes that were commercially successful for them and others is appropriate. Camark, Niloak, and even Weller used some of the same styles during the period, but it does appear that Muncie was the first to market the peachskin glaze, as well as some of the drip glazes, specifically the later white over blue and white over rose varieties. Muncie also developed two unique orange glazes — bittersweet and orange peel — that seem to be different enough from orange glazes used by other companies to give sole credit to Muncie Pottery.

Hand dipping bisque into glaze vat. Drying racks filled with pottery are at rear.

Historians could, and maybe should, argue about what person or company should get credit for a particular glaze, but in the end, it really does not affect the beauty of a particular company's pottery. Since fire destroyed the Muncie records, it is impossible to determine which glazes they developed and which they borrowed. It is equally impossible to determine which glazes others may have borrowed from Muncie and labeled as their own. Muncie's active involvement in glaze development lasted the life of the company. Muncie employees attended conferences, gave lectures, and promoted research and development until the factory closed.

Muncie glazes fall into five categories: 1) early glazes (1922–1925); 2) continuous (1922–late 1930s); 3) sporadic (used here and there over the years); 4) late (1927–late 1930s); 5) experimental or trial glazes of a non-production nature.

The methods used to determine the time periods of various glazes include those available in catalogs (1926, 1929, and #29) and comparisons of early and late shapes with the glazes used on them. A large number of experimental pieces have survived from the late period of the company, and the company may have sold late examples in an effort to recover some of the costs of research and development. Very few, if any, experimental examples that can be traced to the early or middle years exist today. The only experimental pieces attributed to a particular individual are ones created by James Wilkins and still owned by his family. They have his mark, three short parallel lines on the bottom of the pot.

Solid color gloss (or Bright as the catalogs refer to them): Gloss glazes inclued white, black, cobalt blue, medium blue, light blue, mauve-brown, medium green, light green, yellow, brown, maroon, mustard yellow, and plum. Most of these colors were in continuous use, although a few are among the rarest of Muncie glazes. These include white (on early shapes), mauve (on vases), brown, maroon (on early shapes), mustard yellow, and plum.

Gloss (or bright) drip glazes: Gloss drip glazes include cobalt blue over green, light green over white, cobalt blue over white, green over yellow, mauve over white, and dark blue over yellow. The bottoms of early examples have a distinctive look that resembles peachskin. Most of the gloss drip glazes show up on early shapes except green over yellow, found only on much later shapes. Most of these glazes are quite rare, with mauve over white being especially difficult to find.

Peachskin glazes: Peachskin glazes seem to have been in continuous use as examples are found on relatively early shapes as well as late shapes. The color of the drip characterizes bright peachskin glazes. Black, blue, green, or light brown appears over a cream beige base. Also, a peachskin effect appears with no overdrip, just peachskin near the top edges and a creamy beige elsewhere. The amount of peachskin showing through the creamy base varies from piece to piece. It is possible to assemble a variety of pieces in a peachskin glaze that are

Sagger filled with pottery is balanced skillfully on loader's head as he enters kiln.

quite different from each other. Some pieces are completely covered by the peachskin effect, while others have just a spot or two. The fiery rust reds produced through the creamy beige base were due to the migration of iron through the glaze. Kiln temperature was the critical factor, and some pieces are vivid, while others appear faded. Placement within the kiln could also affect the degree of peachskin due to temperature variations within the kiln. A gloss tri-color glaze was available for a while in the early years that resembled black or blue peachskin with red highlights. It differs from the traditional peachskin in the apparent deliberate placement of the red highlights to achieve the three-color effect. All the peachskin varieties have a peachskin-looking residue on the bottom. Blue, black, and to a certain extent, green are fairly common. Light brown peachskin and the tri-color variation are much more difficult to find.

Matte drip glazes: Matte drip combinations used continuously include green over rose, blue over rose, green over lilac, green over pumpkin, green over green, blue over white, rose over white, white over blue, and white over rose. (Analysis of the original glaze books indicates the use of a simple, all-purpose chrome and tin base glaze for the green over rose drip. The tint, rose to green, depended upon its alkaline content.) Early combinations include green over white, blue over white, and rose over white. Most drip glazes were in continuous use except for white over blue and white over rose, which became available in the late 1920s. The continuously used drip combinations are the most common of all the Muncie glazes. The rarest drip combinations are the blue over white and rose over white variations.

Matte brushed glazes: Some drip combination examples had the drip "pulled" down the vase, leaving brush marks that are easily visible on the piece. Later, the technique of actually dipping the vase into a vat of glaze was perfected so brushed examples do not appear for very long. While brushed varieties could exist in any combination, identified examples are of the green over rose, blue over rose, and green over white varieties. While not considered rare, they are not as common as the dripped style and would be earlier examples than the same shape with a drip glaze.

Matte airbrush glazes: Matte airbrush combinations include green over rose and blue over rose. While not as common as the drip varieties, they appear over a number of years.

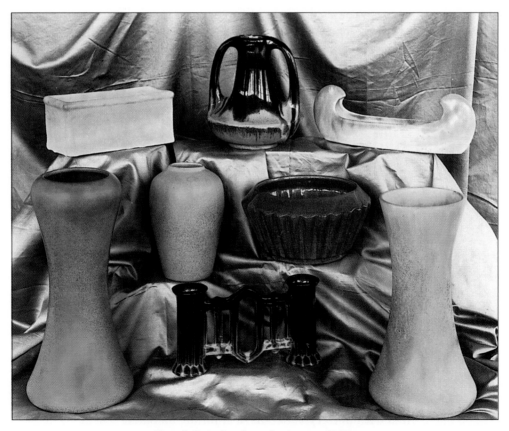

Hand-tinted sales photo, ca. 1927.

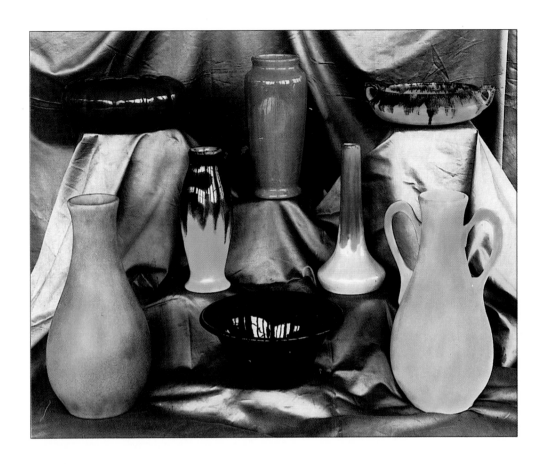

Hand-tinted sales photos, ca. 1927.

Matte tri-glazes: A matte tri-color was in use for a short time in the early years. It consisted of a blended creamy white, blue, and rose. Different looks resulted by purposely not mixing the glazes in a consistent manner. Sometimes the blue shows, sometimes the rose; sometimes both, sometimes neither shows through the creamy white base. The pieces have a creamy white bottom that makes them easy to identify. This creamy white bottom appears only on pieces with this glaze. Often overlooked due to their uncharacteristic appearance, they are not extremely rare.

Solid matte glazes: Solid matte glazes include rose, light green, dark green, dark blue, black (gun metal), and a semi-matte dark green. These seem to have been in use continuously through the years, though not in large numbers like the drip glazes. Rare glazes would include rose and the semi-matte dark green.

Orange glazes: The development of orange peel and bittersweet glazes occurred in the late 1920s or early 1930s. Both were a uranium-based glaze (soda uranate) and are contemporaries of the Cowan oriental red glaze. Bittersweet is darker and has brown to black mottling with a yellow cast, while orange peel is more of a pure orange, with occasional mica-like highlights. Bittersweet is quite rare, except on the juice sets where it seems to be the glaze of choice.

Over the years, Muncie Pottery developed and used some 48 glazes identified by this writer. Look for new discoveries in the next few years, but be careful to include only those glazes used for actual production at the factory. The following photographic examples are just that, examples. Variations in color, density, and other aging factors affect the appearance of glazes. These examples are not the only variations that exist but will help the collector identify the various glazes they might find over a period of time.

MARKINGS

Muncie Pottery is both marked and unmarked. Unmarked examples are usually early pieces dating from 1922–1925 when the pottery was in its beginning stages. Occasionally, examples from this period have shape numbers molded forward or backward into the bottom. A blue "smear" also appears on the bottom of early examples; its purpose is unknown.

Wages based on a piece rate plan that necessitated identifying work done by a particular worker began around 1925. To that end, each worker marked his or her pieces with an assigned number or letter. Finishers used the letters A, B, D, E, K, and M. Molders used Roman numerals I and II as well as 2, 3, 4, and 5. One 6 has surfaced. Molders usually did not work on hand-turned pieces because the finisher did the turning and finishing at the same time. Those pieces have a single mark, normally an A or K. These two finishers seem to have done the majority of hand-turning work, although other marks do turn up from time to time. Pieces marked with just a number mean that for some reason only the molder worked on the piece.

Starting around 1927, workers began stamping the word "MUNCIE" into the bottom of the ware with a die stamp along with the usual letters and numbers. Near the end of production, only the "MUNCIE" stamp was used.

The purpose of a Muncie Pottery stamped mark, along with a similar paper sticker, is unknown, as are the purpose of a unique "hand thrown" ink stamp mark. None are factory production marks. This also is the case with a "tic-tac-toe" type mark that appears on a couple of wall pockets. For some reason, Muncie's eight-sided teapot, creamer, and sugar carry a "300" mark, even though that shape number has proved to be a different vase. Pieces marked by a series of three parallel lines were done for experimental purposes by James Wilkins.

Lamp marks are similar to vase marks, except that many more lamps than vases carry only a single number without an accompanying letter. Lamps made for the Aladdin Co. sometimes carry their die stamp mark by itself or with a Muncie mark.

A stamped, blue ink mark advertising the Charles B. Mayer Company of Indianapolis is routinely found on shape #401. Muncie seems to have been under contract to Mayer to produce quite a few of these vases over the years as they show up more often than the same shape without the advertising mark.

Collectors who limit themselves to only marked pieces are missing a large portion of the pottery's offerings. As a group, early unmarked pieces are the true rarities of the Muncie Pottery, even though some later pieces might bring more money in the market place.

The following photographs are representative of the markings found to date and should help in identifying pieces. Some marks seem to change over the years, such as the 2 or A. Most, if not all, varieties appear in these examples.

VARIETIES OF BASE MARKINGS

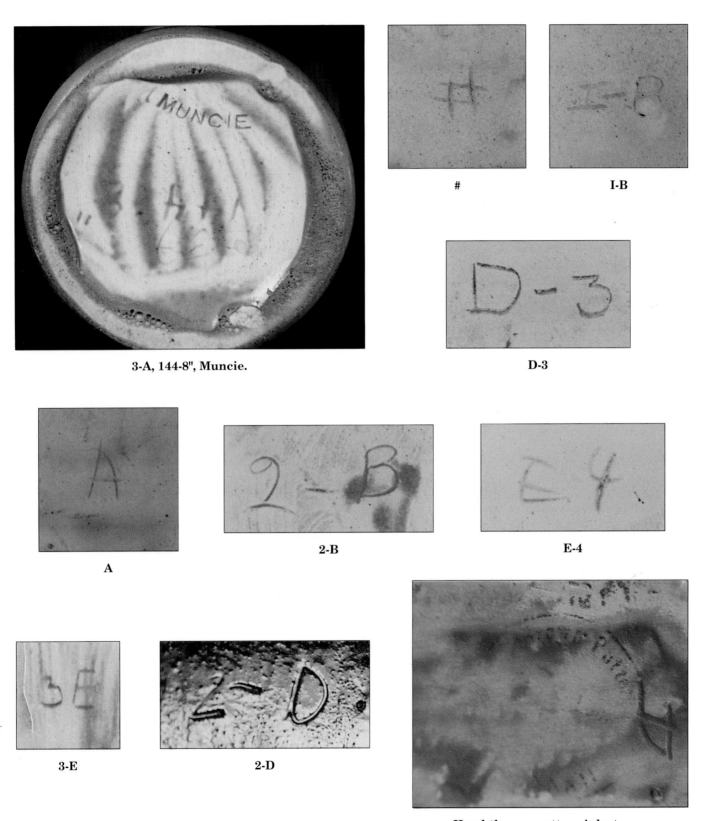

3-A, 144-8", Muncie.

\#

I-B

D-3

A

2-B

E-4

3-E

2-D

Hand-thrown pottery ink stamp.

#300 tea set.

2-B

Round die stamp.

I-A

Round sticker.

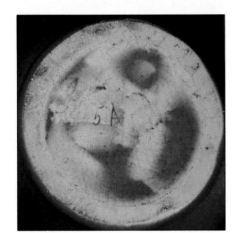

5-A

2-A Muncie.

I-M

100-6", A, Muncie.

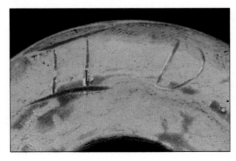

II-D

A variation.

115, 2-B

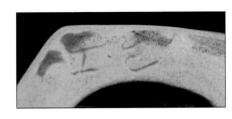

I-E

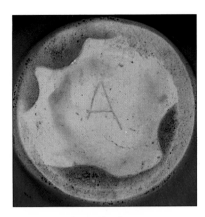

A variation.

I-A

"Muncie Clay Products Co.,
Muncie Indiana" paper label.

K

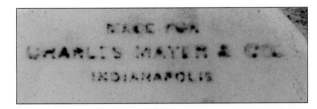

Made for Charles Mayer & Co., Indianapolis, 5-A.

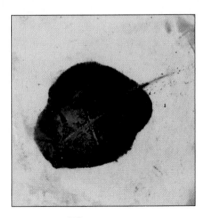

Blue smear.

Aladdin Mfg. No. 415, Muncie, Indiana.

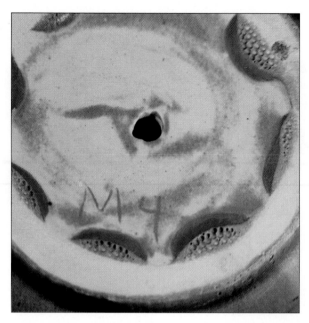

M-4

K-5

I-D

VASES

SHAPE #144

8½", matte white drip over blue, marked Muncie 3A, $100.00–125.00.

6½", matte green drip over white, marked 2D, $70.00–90.00.

12", matte white drip over blue, marked Muncie 1A, $200.00–225.00.

6½", gloss blue peachskin drip, unmarked, $70.00–90.00.

8½", gloss green brushed over white, marked 3, $100.00–125.00.

All size and shape numbers listed are taken from catalogs or marked pieces of pottery. Numbers that begin with "U" are unknown shape numbers and are assigned numbers only to aid in identification. Actual sizes of pottery can vary in height as much as 10-15 percent.

MATTE BLUE OVER ROSE

ROW 1

Shape #250 - 5", airbrushed, unmarked, $325.00−375.00 pair.
Shape #272 - 8", airbrushed, marked 3-?, $70.00−90.00.
Shape #250 - 5", airbrushed, unmarked, $325.00−375.00 pair.

ROW 2

Shape #141 - 9", airbrushed, marked 2D, $250.00−275.00.
Shape #262 - 4½", airbrushed, marked 4, $125.00−150.00.
Shape #267 - 9", dripped, marked 3D, $300.00−350.00.

ROW 3

Shape #134 - 10", dripped, marked K, $175.00−200.00.
Shape #U-2 - 12", airbrushed, marked 2B, $300.00−350.00.
Shape #225 - 10", dripped, marked 2D, $175.00−200.00.
Shape #120 - 10", dripped, marked 3D, $300.00−350.00.

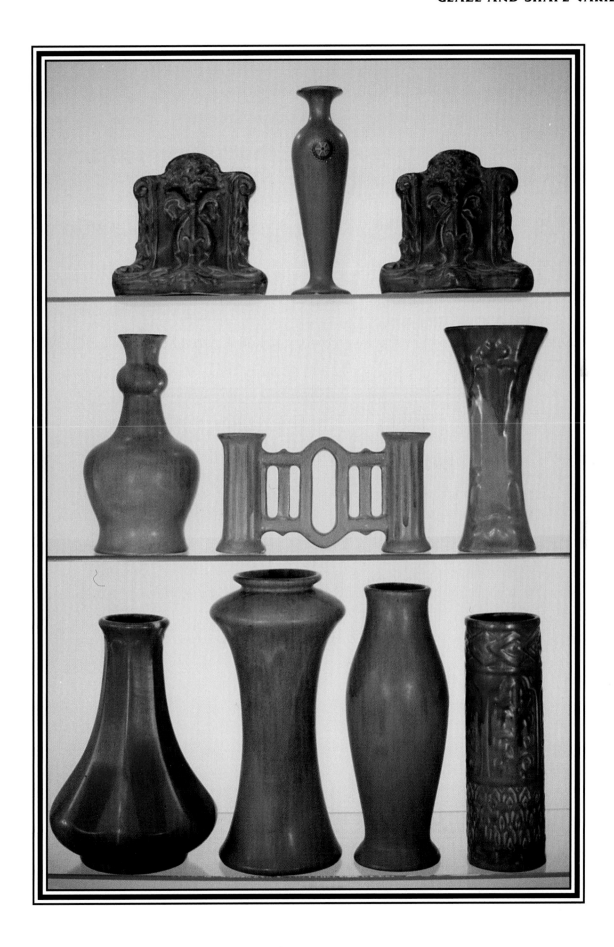

OPPOSITE PAGE

Shape #409 - 12", matte green drip over rose, unmarked, rare shape, $450.00–500.00.

BELOW

Shape #U-3 - 8", matte blue drip over rose, marked ?, rare shape, $250.00–275.00.

MATTE GREEN OVER ROSE

ROW 1

Shape #U-6 - 8", airbrushed, unmarked, $125.00-150.00.
Shape #474 - 6", dripped, marked 5A, with underplate, $300.00-350.00.
  without underplate, $150.00-175.00.
Shape #433 - 6", dripped, marked A, $100.00-125.00.

ROW 2

Shape #U-4 - 8", airbrushed, marked Muncie-3, $225.00-250.00.
Shape #423 - 9", dripped, marked A, $250.00-275.00.
Shape #427 - 7", dripped, marked A, $175.00-200.00.

ROW 3

Shape #215 - 12", airbrushed, marked E4, $250.00-275.00.
Shape #129 - 11", dripped, unmarked, $275.00-300.00.
Shape #122 - 12", airbrushed, unmarked, $250.00-275.00.

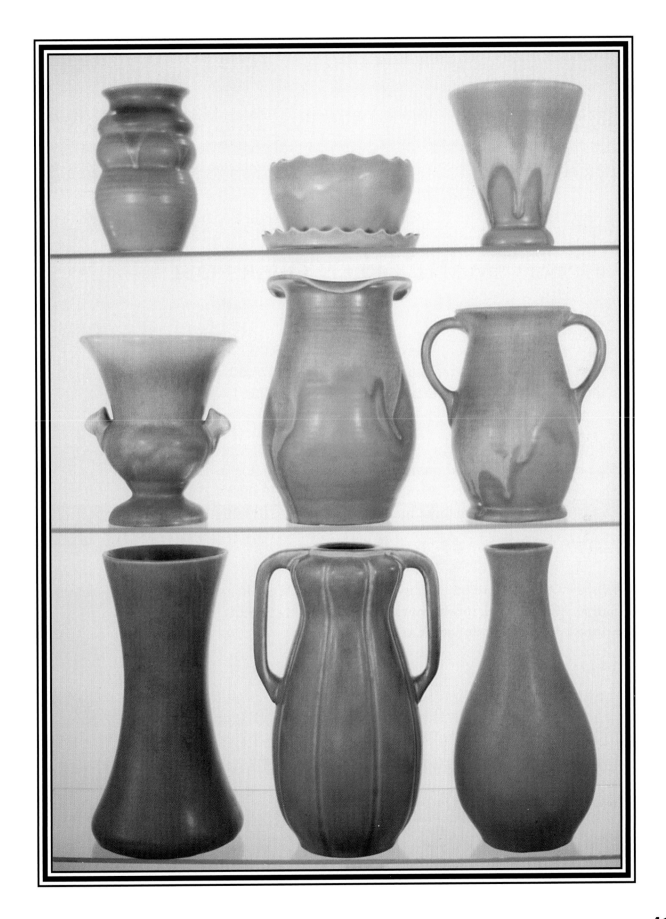

MATTE GREEN OVER ROSE

ROW 1

Shape #102 - 5", dripped, marked 1A, $50.00–70.00.
Shape #464 - 8½", dripped, marked Muncie-A, $275.00–300.00.
Shape #109 - 6", dripped, marked E3, $50.00–70.00.

ROW 2

Shape #402 - 6", dripped, marked K, $125.00–150.00.
Shape #173 - 8", dripped, unmarked, $150.00–175.00.
Shape #466 - 5", airbrushed, marked Muncie-5, $100.00–125.00.

ROW 3

Shape #119 - 12", pulled with a brush, marked 1D, (blue smear), $225.00–250.00.
Shape #100 - 12", dripped, marked 2A, $225.00–250.00.
Shape #401 - 13", dripped, marked 3A, $275.00–300.00.

Shape #190 - 7½", green drip over rose, marked 4, $225.00 – 250.00.

Left: Shape #424 - 12", green drip over rose, marked 2A, $250.00–275.00.
Right: Shape #424 - 18", green drip over green, marked A, rare size, $400.00–450.00.

MATTE GREEN OVER GREEN

ROW 1

Shape #176 - 8", dripped, marked Muncie-3A, $175.00−200.00.
Shape #416 - 7½", dripped, marked A, $250.00−275.00.

ROW 2

Shape #400 - 9", dripped, unmarked, $175.00−200.00.
Shape #U-5 - 6", dripped, marked A, $100.00−125.00.
Shape #420 - 7½", dripped, marked A, $150.00−175.00.

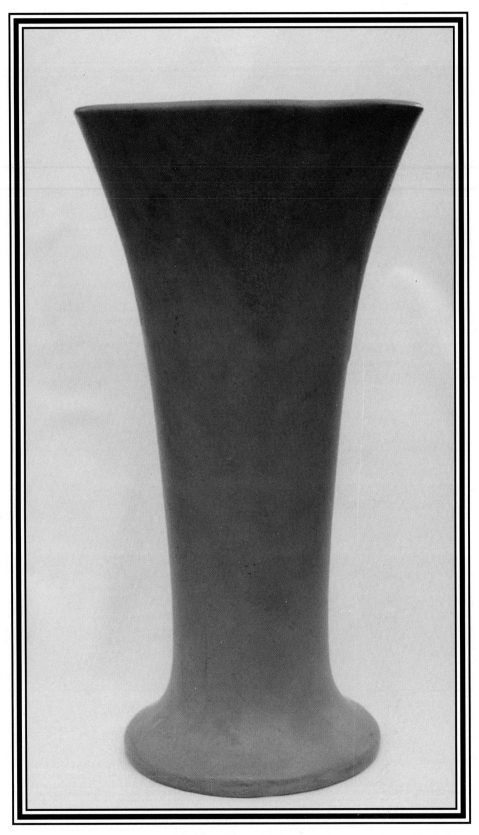

Shape #259 - 12", matte green over green drip, marked 2A, $225.00–250.00.

Shape #460 - 12", green drip over pumpkin, marked 5A,
$300.00–350.00.

MATTE GREEN OVER PUMPKIN

ROW 1

Shape #430 - 7", dripped, marked A, $150.00 – 175.00.
Shape #413 - 4", hand turned, dripped, marked K, $50.00 – 70.00.
Shape #441 - 6½", (variety 2), dripped, marked Muncie-2A, $100.00 – 125.00.

ROW 2

Shape #410 - 6", dripped, marked A, $150.00 – 175.00.
Shape #417 - 6", dripped, marked A, $150.00 – 175.00.

ROW 3

Shape #102 - 9", dripped, unmarked. $150.00 – 175.00.
Shape #404 - 6", (molded), dripped, marked Muncie 1A, $60.00 – 80.00.
Shape #192 - 9", dripped, marked 2A, $150.00 – 175.00.

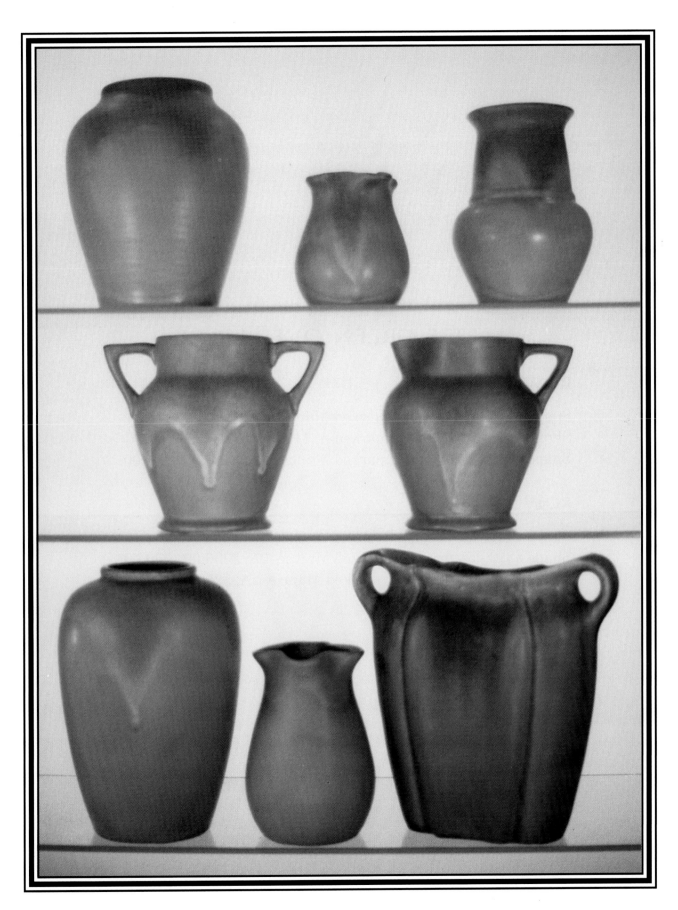

MATTE GREEN OVER LILAC

ROW 1

Shape #U-4 - 8", dripped, marked Muncie-1, $225.00–250.00.
Shape #261 - 9", dripped, marked A, $150.00–175.00.
Shape #182 - 8", dripped, marked Muncie-2A, $150.00–175.00.

ROW 2

Shape #463 - 12", dripped marked A, $225.00–250.00.
Shape #312 - 5", dripped, marked Muncie-3A, $300.00–350.00.
Shape #424 - 12", dripped, marked Muncie-2A, $250.00–275.00.

MATTE GREEN OVER LILAC

ROW 1

Shape #U-5 - 6", dripped, marked A, $100.00–125.00.
Shape #421 - 9", dripped marked A, $300.00–350.00.
Shape #404 - 6", (hand turned), dripped, marked K5, $70.00–90.00.

ROW 2

Shape #191 - 9", dripped, unmarked, $175.00–200.00.
Shape #411 - 5½", dripped, marked 1A, $125.00–150.00.
Shape #416 - 7½", airbrushed, unmarked, $250.00–275.00.

ROW 3

Shape #429 - 6", dripped, marked A, $225.00–250.00.
Shape #410 - 6", dripped, marked A, $150.00–175.00.
Shape #419 - 5", dripped, marked K, $80.00–100.00.

OPPOSITE PAGE

Shape #137 - 11", gloss green drip over white, marked 1, $300.00–350.00.

MATTE AND GLOSS GREEN OVER WHITE

ROW 1

Shape #108 - 6", gloss airbrushed, marked 3-?, $60.00–80.00.

Shape #253 - 11½", gloss pulled with a brush, marked 2D, $275.00–325.00 with frog; $200.00–225.00 without frog.

Shape #102 - 5", gloss airbrushed, marked 4, $50.00–70.00.

ROW 2

Shape #123 -12", matte dripped, marked 1D, $350.00–400.00.

Shape #144 - 6½", matte dripped, marked 2D, $70.00–90.00.

Shape #134 - 7", matte dripped, marked 3D, $125.00–150.00.

Shape #144 - 8½", gloss airbrushed, marked 3-?, $100.00–125.00.

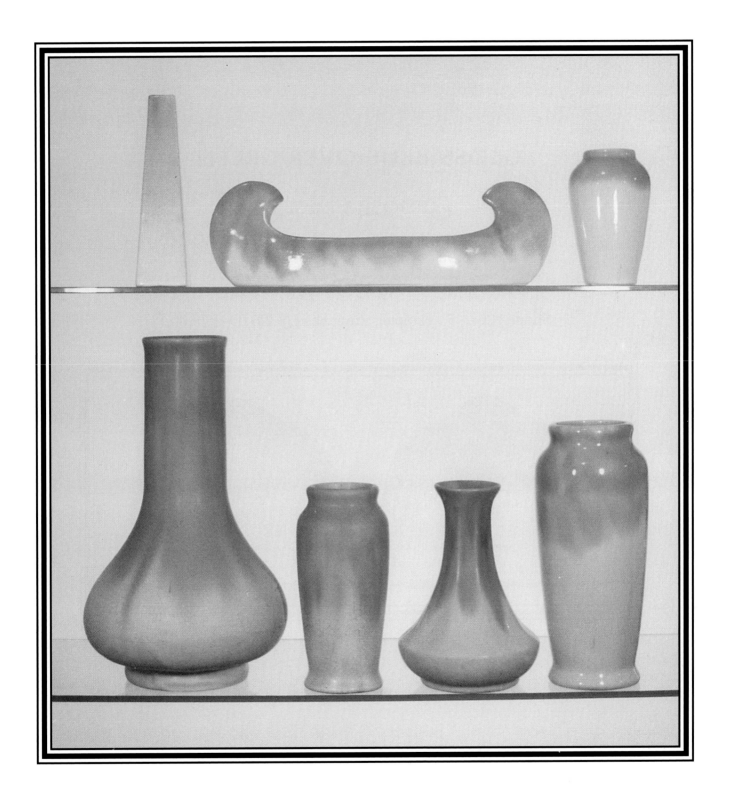

GLOSS BLUE OVER GREEN

OPPOSITE PAGE

Shape #129 - 11", dripped, unmarked, $275.00–300.00.

BELOW

Shape #254 - 5", dripped, unmarked, $325.00–375.00.

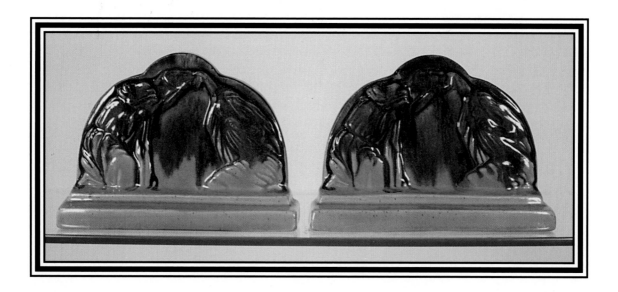

MATTE AND GLOSS BLUE OVER GREEN

ROW 1

Shape #426 - 5", matte dripped, (streaks of white in glaze), marked A, $275.00–300.00.
Shape #447 - 3", matte dripped, unmarked, $150.00–175.00.
Shape #126 - 12", gloss dripped, unmarked, $225.00–250.00.

ROW 2

Shape #187 - 12", gloss airbrushed, unmarked, $100.00–125.00.
Shape #432 - 7", matte dripped, marked A, $225.00–250.00.

ROW 3

Shape #430 - 7", matte dripped, marked A, $150.00–175.00.
Shape #102 - 7", gloss dripped, (appears darker due to crazing), marked 1D, $100.00–125.00.
Shape #431 - 8", matte airbrushed, marked A, $225.00–250.00.

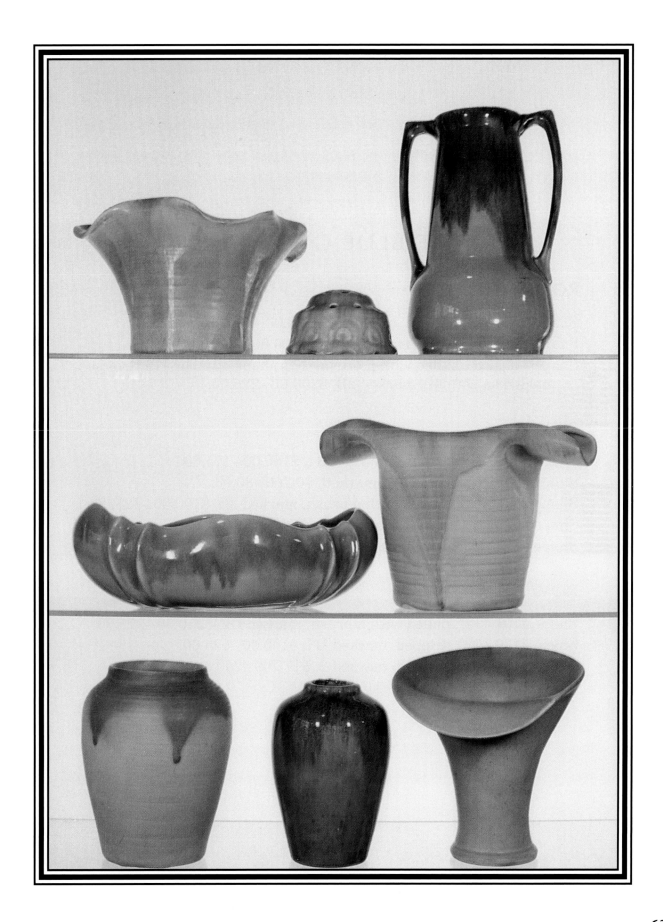

MATTE BLUE OVER WHITE

ROW 1

Shape #105 - 6", dripped, unmarked, $80.00–100.00.

Shape #143 - 7", dripped, marked B4, $100.00–125.00.

Shape #115 - 6", pulled with a brush, (has shape number 115 reverse molded on bottom), marked 2B, $200.00–225.00.

ROW 2

Shape #100 - 10", dripped, marked B4, $150.00–175.00.

Shape #108 - 6", dripped, unmarked, $60.00–80.00.

Shape #144 - 8½", pulled with a brush, marked 3B, $100.00–125.00.

Shape #108 - 6", dripped, marked 1D, $60.00–80.00.

Shape #119 - 9", pulled with a brush, marked 1B, $150.00–175.00.

ROW 3

Shape #101 - 12", pulled with a brush, marked D2, $250.00–275.00.

Shape #136 - 12", dripped, marked D3, $100.00–125.00.

Shape #134 - 10", dripped, marked 2, $175.00–200.00.

OPPOSITE PAGE

Shape #U-7 - 13½", gloss cobalt drip over white with rust highlights showing through, marked D3, rare, $1,200.00+.

GLOSS MAUVE OVER WHITE

ABOVE LEFT

Shape #107 - 6", pulled with a brush, marked 3, $60.00–80.00.

ABOVE RIGHT

Shape #108 - 6", dripped, marked 3, $60.00–80.00.

OPPOSITE PAGE

Shape #129 - 11", pulled with a brush, unmarked, $275.00–300.00.

GLOSS BLUE OVER WHITE

ROW 1

Shape #181 - 7½", dripped, marked 1, $175.00–200.00.

ROW 2

Shape #259 - 9", pulled with a brush, marked D3, $150.00–175.00.
Shape #126 - 12", airbrushed, marked A, $225.00–250.00.
Shape #120 - 10", dripped, marked 1D, $300.00–350.00.

MATTE WHITE OVER ROSE

ROW 1

Shape #113 - 3½", dripped, marked Muncie - 5, $40.00 – 60-00.
Shape #187 - 12", dripped, marked Muncie - 2A, $100.00 – 125.00.

ROW 2

Shape #417 - 6", dripped, marked Muncie - 1A, $150.00 – 175.00.
Shape #403 - 4", dripped, marked 3A, $70.00 – 90.00.
Shape #192 - 6", dripped, marked Muncie - 1A, $80.00 – 100.00.

ROW 3

Shape #445 - 7", dripped, marked Muncie - 1A, $100.00 – 125.00.
Shape #259 - 9", dripped, marked Muncie - 2A, $150.00 – 175.00.
Shape #446 - 8", dripped, marked Muncie - 1A, $125.00 – 150.00.

MATTE WHITE OVER BLUE

Shape #472 - 6", dripped, marked 5A, $100.00–125.00.
Shape #472 - 4", dripped, marked A, $40.00–60.00.
Shape #472 - 12", dripped, (rare size not listed in catalog), marked 5A, $400.00–450.00.

MATTE WHITE OVER BLUE

ROW 1

Shape #442 - 7", dripped, marked Muncie-2A, $125.00–150.00.
Shape #176 - 8", dripped, marked Muncie-1A, $175.00–200.00.
Shape #441 - 6½", (variety 1), dripped, marked Muncie, $100.00–125.00.

ROW 2

Shape #489 - 5½", dripped, marked Muncie-5A, $80.00–100.00.
Shape #432 - 5", dripped, marked A, $150.00–175.00.
Shape #412 - 4½", dripped, marked 5A, $50.00–70.00.

ROW 3

Shape #192 - 9", dripped, marked Muncie-3A, $150.00–175.00.
Shape #107 - 6", dripped, marked 2A, $60.00–80.00.
Shape #418 - 7", dripped, marked A, $225.00–250.00.

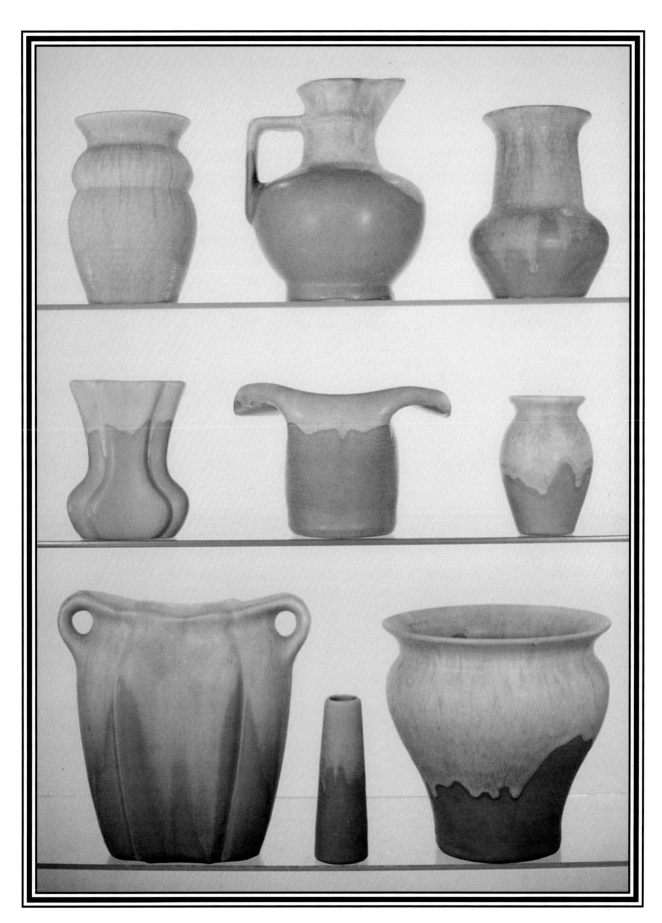

GLOSS PEACHSKIN

OPPOSITE PAGE

Shape #128 - 12", blue drip, unmarked, $350.00–400.00.

BELOW

Shape #254 - 5", green drip, unmarked, $325.00–375.00 pair.

GLOSS PEACHSKIN

ROW 1

Shape #427 - 7", blue drip, marked A, $175.00–200.00.
Shape #415 - 6", blue drip, marked Muncie, $125.00–150.00.
Shape #272 - 8", blue drip, marked 1, $70.00–90.00.
Shape #441 - 6½", (Variety 1), blue drip, marked Muncie-2, $100.00–125.00.

ROW 2

Shape #100 - 6", blue drip, marked 1B, $60.00–80.00.
Shape #111 - 5", blue drip, marked II, $125.00–150.00.
Shape #105 - 6", blue drip, marked 1?, $80.00–100.00.
Shape #413 - 4", (hand turned), blue drip, unmarked, $50.00–70.00.
Shape #107 - 6", blue drip, marked Muncie-5A, $60.00–80.00.

ROW 3

Shape #101 - 12", blue drip, marked 1D, $250.00–275.00.
Shape #U-8 - 8", blue drip, marked Muncie-A1, $150.00–175.00.
Shape #174 - 12", blue drip, unmarked, $600.00–700.00.

GLOSS PEACHSKIN

ROW 1

Shape #192 - 6", black drip, marked Muncie, $80.00–100.00.
Shape #119 - 9", blue drip, marked 1D, $150.00–175.00.
Shape #488 - 5", black drip, unmarked, $80.00–100.00.

ROW 2

Shape #480 - 3½", black drip, marked Muncie-2A, $70.00–90.00.
Shape #262 - 4¼", blue drip, unmarked, $125.00–150.00.
Shape #113 - 3½", black drip, marked 5A, $40.00–60.00.

ROW 3

Shape #484 - 7", black drip, marked Muncie-2A, $175.00–200.00.
Shape #464 - 8½", black drip, marked Muncie-1A, $275.00–300.00.
Shape #479 - 7", black drip, marked 3A, $100.00–125.00.

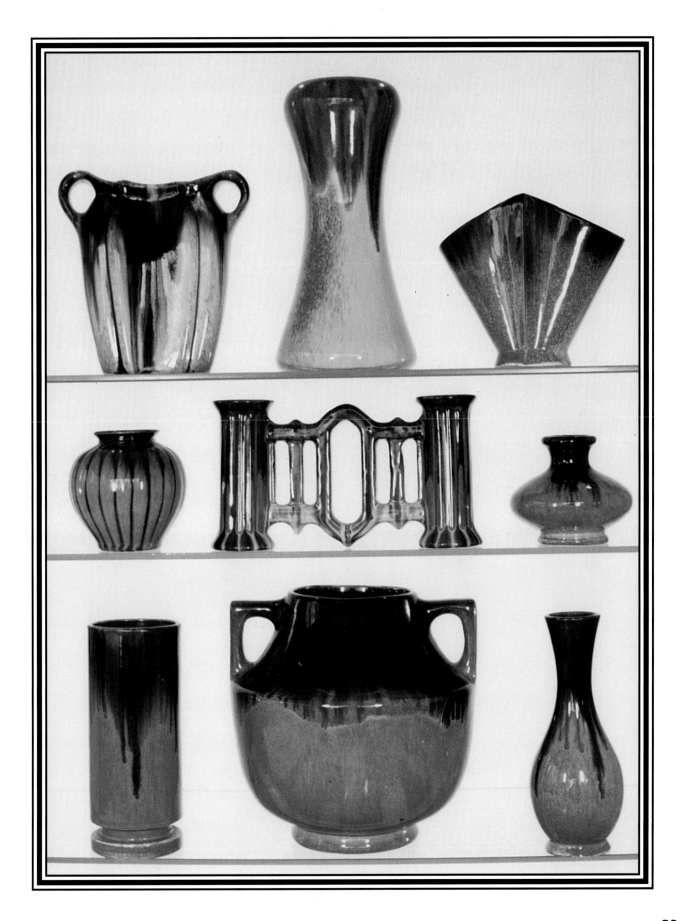

Shape #124 - 12", light brown drip peachskin, marked 1D, rare, $450.00−500.00.

Shape #121 - 12", light brown drip peachskin, unmarked, $400.00–450.00.

GLOSS PEACHSKIN

ROW 1

Shape #149 - 6", tri-color drip, unmarked, $225.00–250.00 pair.
Shape #104 - 8", tri-color drip, marked 5, $80.00–100.00.
Shape #152 - 3", light brown drip, unmarked, $125.00–150.00.
Shape #106 - 7", light brown drip, marked 3D, $100.00–125.00.
Shape #149 - 6", tri-color drip, unmarked, $225.00–250.00 pair.

ROW 2

Shape #253 - 11½", green drip, marked 3D, $275.00–325.00 with frog;
  $200.00–225.00 without frog.
Shape #257 - 5", light brown drip, unmarked, $300.00–350.00 pair.

ROW 3

Shape #261 - 9", tri-color drip, marked 1M, $150.00–175.00.
Shape #109 - 6", light brown drip, marked 1D, $50.00–70.00.
Shape #259 - 9", light brown drip, marked D3, $150.00–175.00
Shape #119 - 6", tri-color drip, marked D3, $60.00–80.00.
Shape #100 - 8", green drip, marked 3D, $100.00–125.00.

MATTE TRI-COLOR

ROW 1

Shape #185 - 12", dripped, unmarked, $225.00 – 250.00.
Shape #258 - 7", dripped, unmarked, $225.00 – 250.00.

ROW 2

Shape #186 - 7", dripped, unmarked, $125.00 – 150.00.
Shape #116 - 3½", airbrushed, marked 1, $40.00 – 60.00.
Shape #111 - 5", airbrushed, unmarked, $125.00 – 150.00.
Shape #117 - 3½", airbrushed, unmarked, $40.00 – 60.00.
Shape #144 - 6½", airbrushed, marked B4, $70.00 – 90.00.

GUNMETAL BLACK

ROW 1

Shape #466 - 5", semi-matte, marked 3A, $100.00–125.00.
Shape #403 - 4", semi-matte, marked 2A, $70.00–90.00.
Shape #191 - 6", semi-matte, marked Muncie, $80.00–100.00.

ROW 2

Shape #422 - 9", semi-matte, marked A, $175.00–200.00.
Shape #432 - 5", semi-matte, marked 1A, $150.00–175.00.
Shape #463 - 12", semi-matte, marked Muncie-2A, $225.00–250.00.

GLOSS BLACK

ROW 1

Shape #428 - 6", marked A, $80.00–100.00.
Shape #U-9 - 6", marked 3D, $225.00–250.00.
Shape #404 - 6", molded variety, marked 1A, $60.00–80.00.

ROW 2

Shape #495 - 4", marked Muncie-3, $60.00–80.00.
Shape #169 - 9", unmarked, $150.00–175.00.
Shape #468 - 4", marked Muncie, $70.00–90.00.

ROW 3

Shape #136 - 12", marked Muncie-1, $100.00–125.00.
Shape #238 - 9", marked 5A, $125.00–150.00.
Shape #177 - 7", marked Muncie-3A, $125.00–150.00.

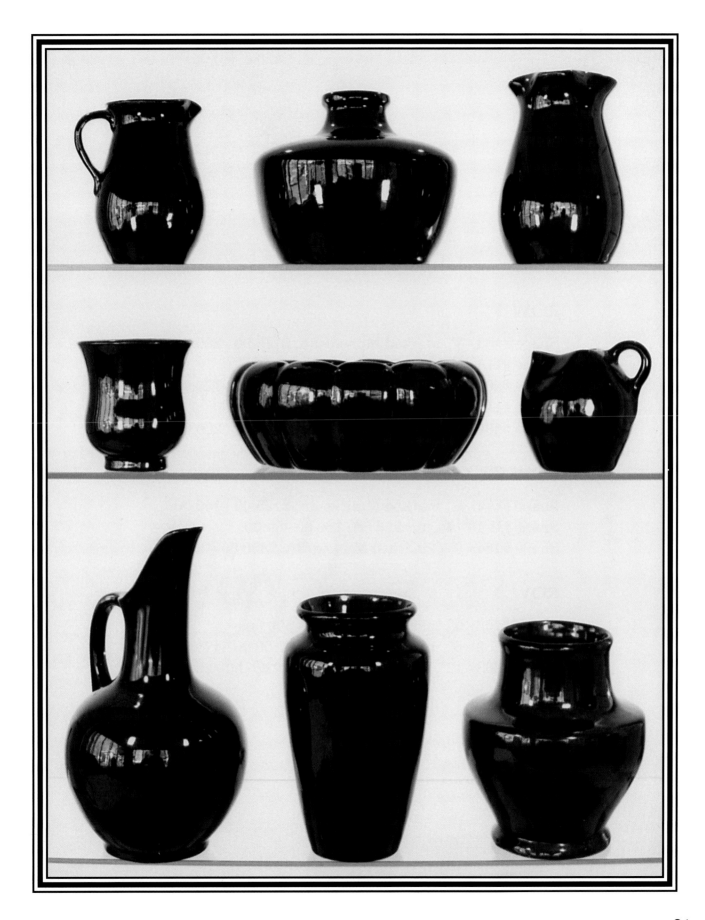

ORANGE PEEL

ROW 1

Shape #483 - 7", marked Muncie-5A, $175.00–200.00.
Shape #118 - 3½", marked 4, $40.00–60.00.
Shape #261 - 9", marked Muncie-3A, $150.00–175.00.
Shape #117 - 3½", marked Muncie-A, $40.00–60.00.
Shape #484 - 7", marked Muncie-3A, $175.00–200.00.

ROW 2

Shape #415 - 6", marked Muncie-3A, $125.00–150.00.
Shape #U-10 - 4", marked 5A, $60.00–80.00.
Shape #194 - 6½", marked Muncie-5A, $300.00–350.00.

ROW 3

Shape #408 - 9", marked A, $275.00–300.00.
Shape #U-8 - 8", marked Muncie-5A, $150.00–175.00.
Shape #463 - 12", marked Muncie-1A, $225.00–250.00.

MATTE BITTERSWEET ORANGE

Shape #181 - 7½", dripped, marked Muncie-1A, $175.00–200.00.

DARK MATTE GREEN

ROW 1

Shape #118 - 3½", dripped, marked 3, $40.00–60.00.
Shape #119 - 6", dripped, marked 4, $60.00–80.00.
Shape #192 - 6", dripped, unmarked, $80.00–100.00.
Shape #412 - 4½", dripped, unmarked, $50.00–70.00.

ROW 2

Shape #104 - 8", dripped, marked E4, $80.00–100.00.
Shape #253 - 11½", dripped, unmarked, $275.00–325.00 with frog;
    $200.00–225.00 without frog.
Shape #112 - 8", dripped, marked 1, $100.00–125.00.

DARK MATTE BLUE

ROW 1

Shape #185 - 7", unmarked, $200.00–225.00.
Shape #102 - 7", marked 4, $100.00–125.00.
Shape #116 - 3½", marked 4, $40.00–60.00.

ROW 2

Shape #238 - 5", marked 4, $60.00–80.00.
Shape #169 - 7", marked 1E, $100.00–125.00.
Shape #145 - 4", marked 4, $100.00–125.00.

ROW 3

Shape #186 - 7", unmarked, $125.00–150.00.
Shape #119 - 9", marked 1E, $150.00–175.00.
Shape #102 - 9", marked 3E, $150.00–175.00.

GLOSS BLUE VARIATIONS

ROW 1

Shape #104 - 8", gloss cobalt blue, unmarked, $80.00–100.00.
Shape #100 - 12", gloss light blue, marked 3E, $225.00–250.00.
Shape #134 - 10", gloss cobalt blue, unmarked, $175.00–200.00.

ROW 2

Shape #181 - 7½", gloss light blue, marked 3E, $175.00–200.00.
Shape #104 - 8", gloss medium blue, unmarked, $80.00–100.00.
Shape #134 - 7", gloss medium blue, marked 3, $125.00–150.00.
Shape #238 - 9", gloss light blue, marked Muncie-1, $125.00–150.00.

ROW 3

Shape #428 - 6", gloss dark blue, marked 2A, $80.00–100.00.
Shape #100 - 6", gloss light blue, marked 1, $60.00–80.00.
Shape #143 - 7", gloss medium blue, marked 1E, $100.00–125.00.
Shape #119 - 6", gloss dark blue, marked 5-?, $60.00–80.00.
Shape #110 - 3½", gloss light blue, marked Muncie-1, $100.00–125.00.

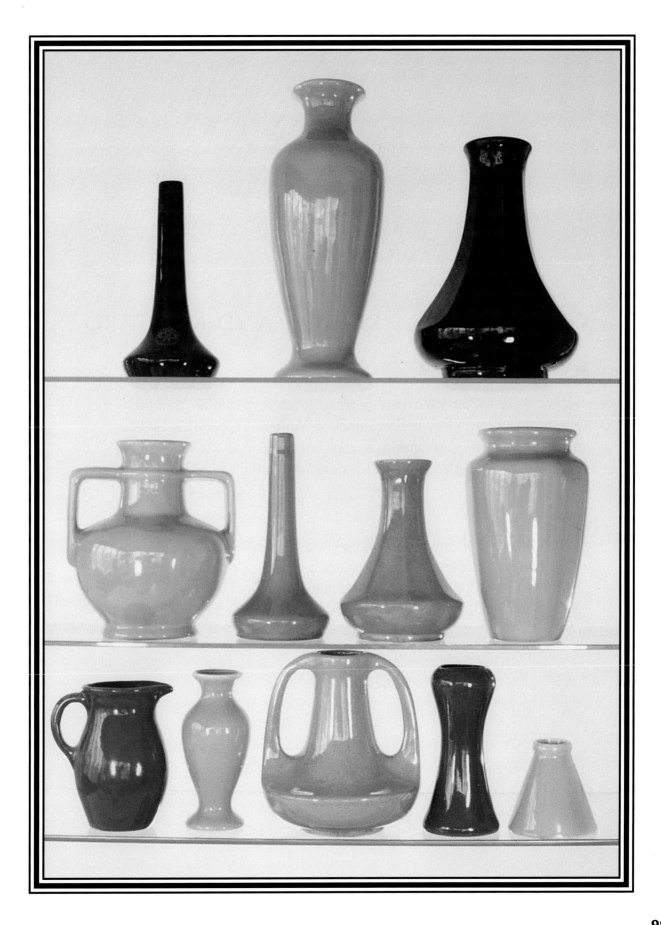

GLOSS GREEN, YELLOW, AND MUSTARD

ROW 1

Shape #479 - 7", gloss green, marked Muncie, $100.00–125.00.
Shape #419 - 5", gloss yellow, marked Muncie-A, $80.00–100.00.
Shape #485 - 5", gloss green, marked Muncie-5, $100.00–125.00.
Shape #112 - 8", gloss yellow, unmarked, $100.00–125.00.

ROW 2

Shape #401 - 13", gloss yellow, marked 5A, (ink stamp on bottom
    advertising Mayer Co., Indianapolis, Ind.), $275.00–300.00.
Shape #134 - 7", gloss mustard yellow, unmarked, $125.00–150.00.
Shape #478 - 12", gloss green, marked Muncie-A, $300.00–350.00.

GLOSS GREENS AND YELLOWS

ROW 1

Shape #445 - 7", gloss green, marked 2A, $100.00–125.00.
Shape #446 - 8", gloss green drip over yellow, marked Muncie-5A, $125.00–150.00.
Shape #445 - 7", gloss yellow, marked Muncie-2A, $100.00–125.00.

ROW 2

Shape #102 - 7", gloss yellow, marked 1A, $100.00–125.00.
Shape #488 - 5", gloss green, marked Muncie-5, $80.00–100.00.
Shape #192 - 6", gloss yellow, marked Muncie A, $80.00–100.00.

ROW 3

Shape #420 - 7½", gloss green drip over yellow, marked Muncie-5A, $150.00–175.00.
Shape #177 - 7", semi-gloss mustard yellow, unmarked, $125.00–150.00.
Shape #422 - 9", gloss green, marked A, $175.00–200.00.

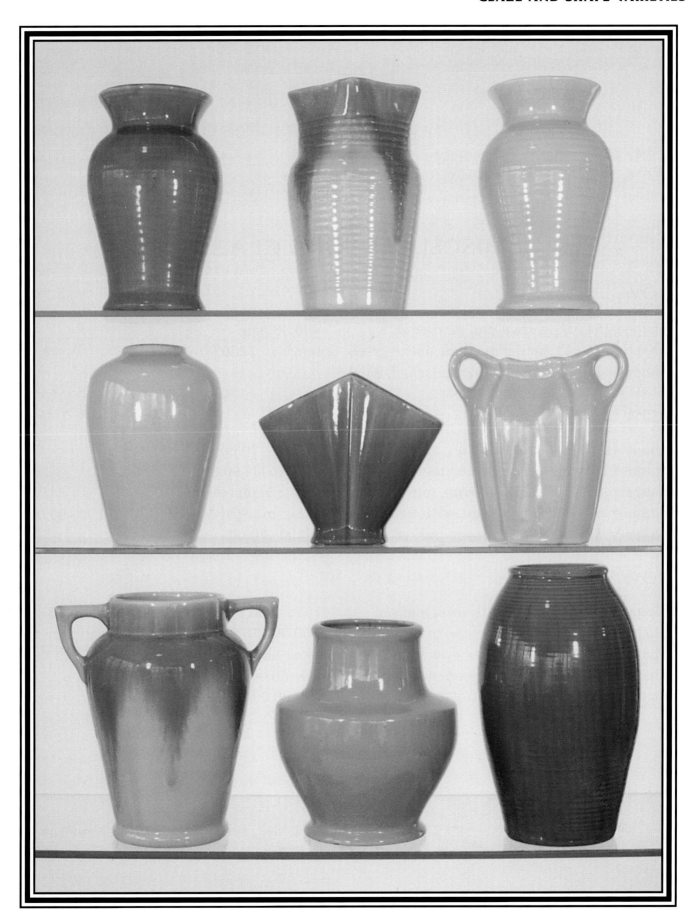

MISCELLANEOUS GLAZES

ROW 1

Shape #154 - 9", gloss plum, marked 3, $350.00–400.00 pair.
Shape #278 - 5", semi-gloss dark matte green, unmarked, $250.00–275.00.
Shape #154 - 9", gloss plum, unmarked, $350.00–400.00 pair.

ROW 2

Shape #U-11 - 3", gloss maroon, marked Muncie, $50.00–70.00.
Shape #480 - 3½", gloss white, marked Muncie-5A, $70.00–90.00.
Shape #480 - 3½", gloss maroon, marked Muncie-5A, $70.00–90.00.
Shape #480 - 3½", gloss white with light blue speckles, marked Muncie-5A, $70.00–90.00.
Shape U-12 - 3", gloss maroon, marked Muncie, $50.00–70.00.

ROW 3

Shape #115 - 6", matte light rose, marked and #115 molded on bottom, $200.00–225.00.
Shape #U-13 - 3½", gloss white, marked Muncie, $50.00–70.00.
Shape #168 - 3", matte green over lime green, marked 3E, $60.00–80.00.
Shape #113 - 3½", gloss maroon, marked 2-?, $40.00–60.00.
Shape #485 - 5", gloss maroon, marked Muncie-A, $100.00–125.00.

MISCELLANEOUS GLAZES

ROW 1

Shape #404 - 6", (molded), part gloss/part matte black, marked Muncie-1A, $60.00–80.00.

Shape #490 - 4", light blue matte, marked Muncie-1, $125.00–150.00.

Shape #402 - 6", matte dark gray, marked A, $125.00–150.00.

ROW 2

Shape #U-14 - 4", olive green semi-gloss, marked Muncie, $60.00–80.00.

Shape #312 - 5", olive green semi-gloss, marked Muncie, $300.00–350.00.

Shape #413 - 4", (molded), gloss cobalt over yellow, marked 5A, $40.00–60.00.

ROW 3

Shape #225 - 8", gloss creamy yellow with rust highlights, "225" molded backwards on bottom, unmarked, $125.00–150.00.

Shape #215 - 12", green airbrush over gloss maroon, marked 1E, $250.00–275.00.

Shape #100 - 8", gloss mauve-brown, unmarked, $100.00–125.00.

GLOSS AND MATTE GLAZES

TOP PHOTO

Shape #468 - 4", gloss white, marked Muncie, $70.00–90.00.
Shape #258 - 7", gloss white, marked Muncie, $225.00–250.00.
Shape #U-10 - 4", gloss white, marked Muncie, $60.00–80.00.

MIDDLE PHOTO

Shape #U-15 - 5", gloss red-orange, (late experimental shape and glaze), marked Muncie, $70.00–90.00.
Shape #U-16 - 4", gloss light blue exterior and gloss white interior, (late experimental shape and glaze, smaller version of a known radio lamp shape), marked Muncie, $70.00–90.00.

BOTTOM PHOTO

Shape #U-17 - 4", olive green semi-gloss, rough texture, (late experimental shape and glaze), marked Muncie, $70.00–90.00.

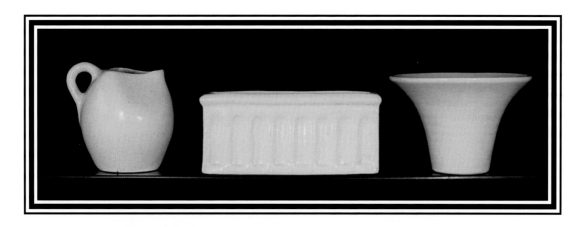

WALL POCKETS

ROW 1

Shape #266 - 9", matte green airbrush over rose, marked 3E, $275.00–300.00.
Shape #200 - 6", matte green drip over green, marked with a tic-tac-toe figure, $225.00–250.00.
Shape #266 - 9", matte green airbrush over rose, marked 1D, $275.00–300.00.

ROW 2

Shape #252 - 10", matte green airbrush over rose, marked 1E, $250.00–275.00.
Shape #200 - 3½", matte green airbrush over rose, marked E4, $200.00–225.00.
Shape #252 - 10", gloss light brown peachskin, marked 2D, $250.00–275.00.

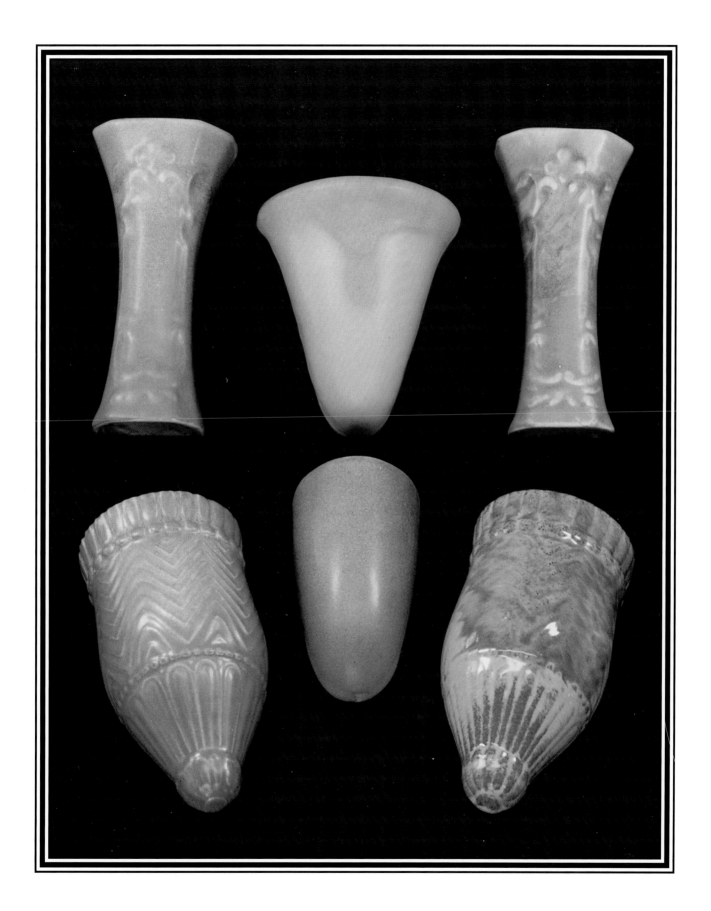

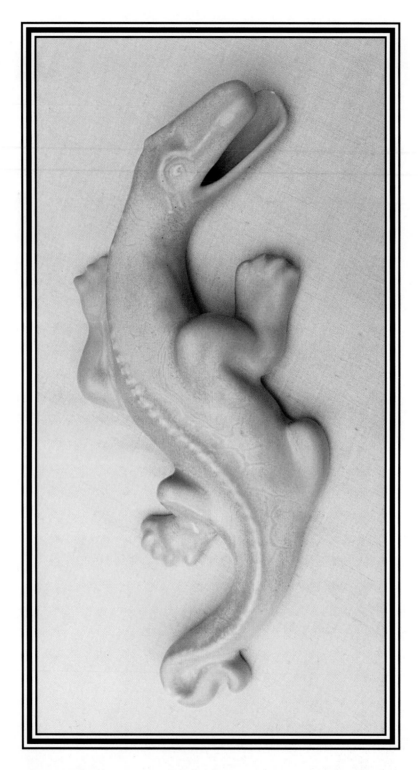

Shape #251 - 9", highly desirable salamander wall pocket, green airbrush over rose, unmarked, $1,000.00+.

CANDLESTICKS

Shape #U-18 - 8", early candlestick, blue drip over rose, unmarked, $225.00 – 250.00.

ROW 1

Shape #145 - 4", matte green drip over rose, marked E4, $100.00−125.00 single.
Shape #154 - 9", matte blue drip over rose, marked M4, $350.00−400.00 pair.
Shape #155 - 13", gloss blue peachskin, unmarked, $300.00−350.00 single.
Shape #154 - 9", matte blue drip over rose, marked M4, $350.00−400.00 pair.
Shape #145 - 4", matte green drip over rose, marked 4, $100.00−125.00 single.

ROW 2

Shape #150 - 9", matte green drip over rose, marked 3B, $275.00−300.00 pair.
Shape #149 - 6", matte blue drip over white, marked 2B, $225.00−250.00 pair.
Shape #196 - 4", matte green drip over rose, unmarked, $70.00−90.00 pair.
Shape #195 - 8", matte green airbrush over rose, unmarked. $200.00−225.00 single.
Shape #196 - 4", matte green drip over rose, unmarked, $70.00−90.00 pair.
Shape #149 - 6", matte blue drip over white, unmarked, $225.00−250.00 pair.
Shape #150 - 9", matte green drip over rose, marked 1, $275.00−300.00 pair.

CANDLESTICKS AND CONSOLE SETS

ROW 1

Shape #414 - 4", matte green drip over lilac, unmarked, $175.00–200.00.
Shape #153 - 3", matte green drip over white, unmarked, $100.00–125.00.
Shape #152 - 3", matte green drip over rose, marked ?D, $125.00–150.00.

ROW 2

Shape #197 - 3½", matte green drip over lilac, marked 1A, $150.00–175.00 pair.
Shape #197 - 3½", matte green drip over lilac, unmarked, $150.00–175.00 pair.
Shape #187 - 12", matte green drip over pumpkin, marked 2A, $100.00–125.00.

ROW 3

Shape #U-19 - 14", matte white drip over blue, marked Muncie-1, $200.00–225.00.
Shape #198 - 2¾", matte green drip over lilac, marked 1A, $175.00–200.00 pair.
Shape #198 - 2¾", matte green drip over lilac, marked 2, $175.00–200.00 pair.

ROW 4

Shape #196 - 4", matte green drip over rose, unmarked, $70.00–90.00 pair.
Shape #185 - 12", matte tri-color drip, unmarked, $225.00–250.00.
Shape #196 - 4", matte green drip over rose, unmarked, $70.00–90.00 pair.

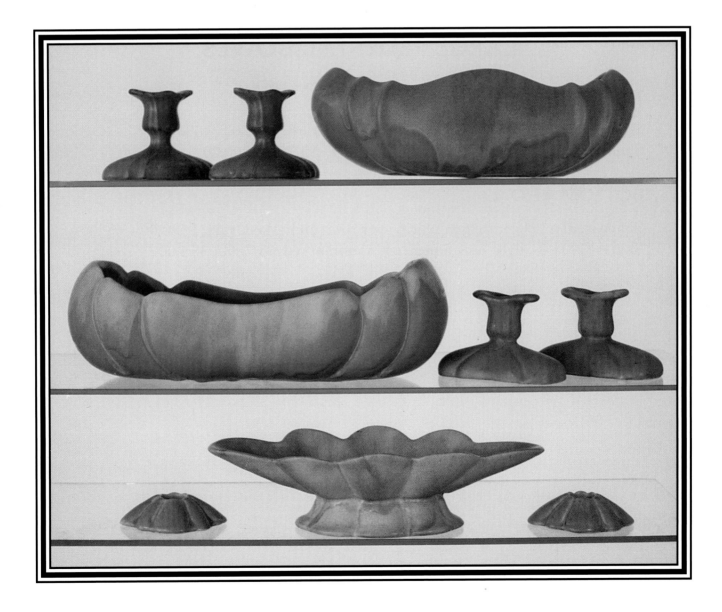

LARGE PEDESTAL BOWLS

TOP PHOTO

Shape #159 - 11", blue peachskin, unmarked, rare, $400.00–450.00.
Shape #183 - 11", blue peachskin, unmarked, $275.00–300.00.

BOTTOM PHOTO

Shape #161 - 12", matte green drip over rose, unmarked, rare, $500.00–550.00.
Shape #173 - 8", light brown peachskin, unmarked, $150.00–175.00.

BOWLS

ROW 1

Shape #169 - 7", matte green drip over rose, marked D3, $100.00 – 125.00.
Shape #170 - 5", matte blue over rose, marked 2B, rare, $225.00 – 250.00.
Shape #265 - 7½", matte green drip over rose, unmarked, (blue smear), $125.00 – 150.00.

ROW 2

Shape #168 - 6", green peachskin, marked 1B, $70.00 – 90.00.
Shape #166 - 7", matte blue drip over rose, marked 1B, $300.00 – 350.00.
Shape #168 - 3", blue peachskin, unmarked, $60.00 – 80.00.

ROW 3

Shape #168 - 9", blue peachskin, marked 2B, $125.00 – 150.00.
Shape #169 - 9", gloss black, unmarked, $150.00 – 175.00.

ROW 1

Shape #179 - 8", matte dark blue, marked 3E, $150.00–175.00.
Shape #157 - 11", matte dark blue, unmarked (blue smear), $200.00–225.00.

ROW 2

Shape #158 - 12", matte blue airbrush over rose, unmarked, $225.00–250.00.
Shape #172 - 8", matte blue drip over rose, marked 1B, $200.00–225.00.

ROW 3

Shape #162 - 8", matte green drip over green, unmarked, $100.00–125.00.
Shape #167 - 11", blue peachskin, unmarked, $200.00–225.00.

FLOWER FROGS

TOP PHOTO

STANDARD FLOWER FROG: Shape #255 - 3" diameter, 1¼" height. Frogs are usually unmarked; however, peachskin example at left center is marked with a "3." These frogs always have 9 holes without a center hole and always have 3 "feet." $30.00–50.00 each.

BOTTOM PHOTO

LARGE FLOWER FROG (left to right): Shape #447 - 4½" diameter, 3" height. This size is rare. These frogs have 21 holes total. Left example marked 2A, right example is unmarked. $150.00–175.00 each.

CANOE FROG (center): Shape #253 - 6¼" length, 2" width, ⅞" height. (Same shape # as canoe vase, not originally sold without canoe.) Usually unmarked with 15 holes and fairly common. Canoe frogs are rarer than canoes. $75.00–100.00.

NOVELTY ITEMS

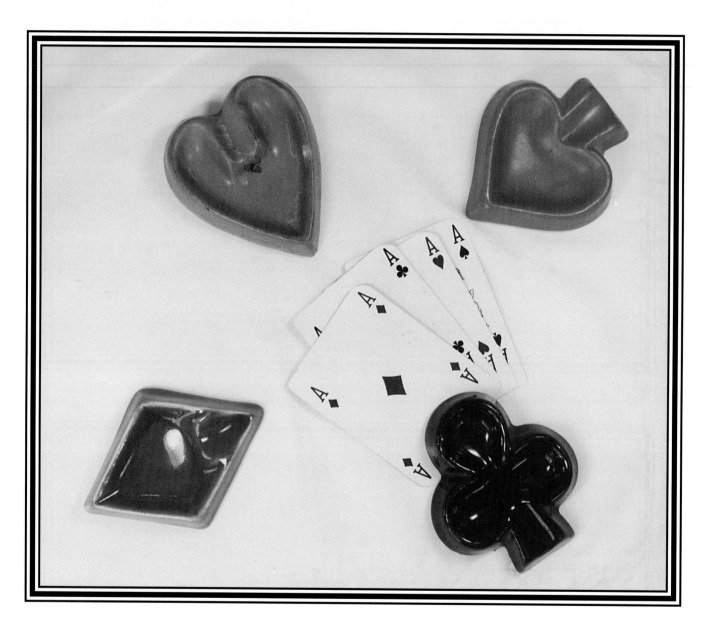

BRIDGE ASHTRAY SET

Shape #270 - 3"–4", various glazes, occasionally marked, $225.00–250.00 set; $50.00–60.00
    individually.

CANDY JARS AND TOBACCO JARS

ROW 1

Shape #271 - 8" (without lid), gloss cobalt drip over green, unmarked, $100.00–125.00 without lid; $225.00–250.00 with lid.

Shape #271 - 8" (without lid), matte blue airbrush over rose, unmarked, $100.00–125.00 without lid; $225.00–250.00 with lid.

Shape #271 - 8" (without lid), matte dark green, unmarked, $100.00–125.00 without lid; $225.00–250.00 with lid.

ROW 2

Shape #268 - 8", matte blue airbrush over rose, marked E4, "268" molded into bottom, rare with lid, $125.00–150.00 without lid; $225.00–250.00 with lid.

Shape #268 - 8", gloss dark blue, unmarked, "268" molded into bottom, rare with lid, $125.00–150.00 without lid; $225.00–250.00 with lid.

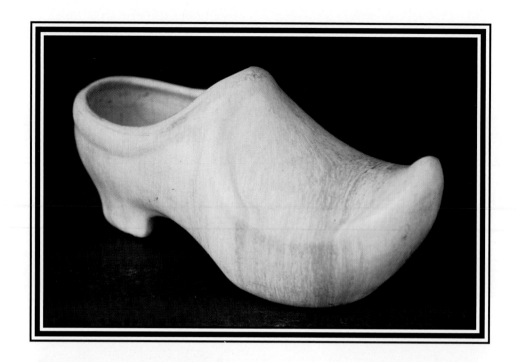

SHOES

TOP PHOTO

Shape #U20 - 5" length, matte white drip over rose, unmarked, $250.00 – 275.00.

BOTTOM PHOTO

Shape #U20 - 5" length, matte green drip over rose, unmarked, $250.00 – 275.00.

ODDS AND ENDS

ROW 1

Shape #U21 - 7", gloss orange peel, marked 2A, $175.00–200.00.
Shape #495 - 4", gloss orange peel, marked 5A, $60.00–80.00.
Shape #U21 - 7", matte green airbrush over rose, marked Muncie-A, $175.00–200.00.

ROW 2

Shape #U22 - 5", gloss white with blue splotches, (trial or playful glaze), unmarked, rare, $250.00–275.00.
Shape #213 - 5½", matte green drip over rose, unmarked, $175.00–200.00.
Shape #U22 - 5", gloss brown, marked Muncie, rare, $250.00–275.00.

ROW 3

Shape #212 - 5", gloss cobalt, marked 4, $175.00–200.00.
Shape #184 - 8", gloss brown, unmarked, rare, $200.00–225.00.
Shape #U23 - 5", matte white drip over blue, unmarked, $175.00–200.00.

ODDS AND ENDS

LEFT

Shape #269 - 5", blue drip over rose, unmarked, (attached base listed in catalog is unknown), $175.00–200.00.

RIGHT

Shape #206 - 4", matte green drip over lilac, unmarked, $150.00–175.00.

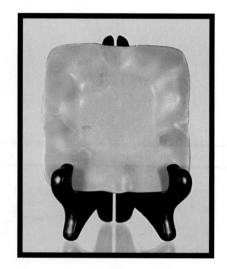

WATER, JUICE, AND TEA SETS

ROW 1

Water Set - Pitcher with 4 cups (rare as a set), $450.00–550.00.
Shape #405 - 5", matte green drip over pumpkin, marked K, $60.00–80.00.
Shape #405 - 5", matte green drip over lilac, marked A, $60.00–80.00.
Shape #405 - 5", matte white drip over blue, marked A, $60.00–80.00.
Shape #406 - 12", matte dark green, marked K, $200.00–225.00.

ROW 2

Juice Set - Pitcher with 6 cups (pitcher and glass have same shape #), $225.00–250.00.
Shape #494 - 4", juice glasses, bittersweet orange, marked either Muncie or A, $20.00–30.00 each.
Shape #494 - 7", juice pitcher, bittersweet orange, marked Muncie, $75.00–100.00.

ROW 3

Tea set - Teapot, creamer, and sugar, extremely rare as a set, (set pictured, missing sugar bowl lid), $450.00–500.00.
Shape #U24, various sizes, all gloss light blue, all pieces except underplate marked #300 on bottom.

PITCHER, MUG, AND MUSIC BOXES

ROW 1

Pitcher and mug set, could be special ordered from the factory for a special occasion.
Shape #U25 - 8", blue peachskin, unmarked, rare, $250.00–275.00.
Shape #U26 - 4", blue peachskin, marked A, rare, $100.00–125.00.

ROW 2

Pitchers with music box bottoms, (rare with original music box intact).
Shape #U27 - 8", gloss medium green, marked 3A, $225.00–250.00 with stopper.
Shape #U28 - 7", gloss light green, unmarked, rare, $275.00–300.00.

ROW 3

Pinch jugs with music box bottoms, (rare with original music box intact).
Shape #U29 - 10", gloss green drip over white, marked 2A, $125.00–150.00 without stopper;
   $225.00–250.00 with stopper.
Shape #U29 - 10", blue peachskin, marked Muncie-5A, $125.00–150.00 without stopper;
   $225.00–250.00 with stopper.

Shape #U30 - 9", music box bottom, gloss brown, marked 3A, $250.00 – 275.00.

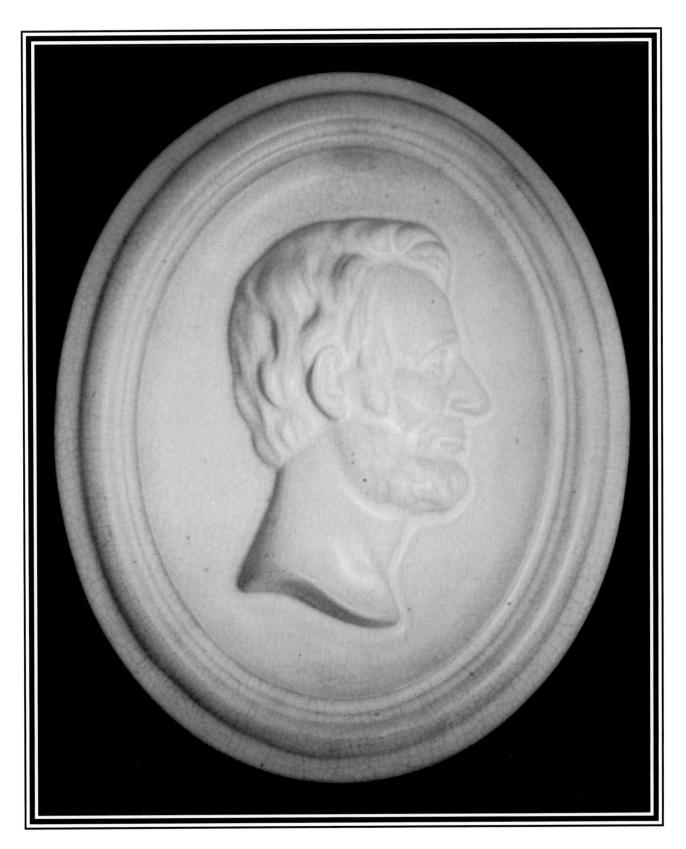

Shape #U31 - 10" oval with Lincoln facing right (also Washington facing left is known), gloss white, unmarked, $300.00–325.00 each.

TEA SET AND TRIVET
MATTE "RED BLUE SPRAY"

TOP PHOTO

Tea set, probably experimental as all the pieces are marked "Red Blue Spray" and 1A, somewhat cruder than normal production pieces, $150.00–200.00 set.

RIGHT, MIDDLE

Tea trivet, probably part of the set above but found in different location, mark pictured below is on the back of this tile, $50.00–75.00.

LEFT, BELOW

Back of tile, mark that appears on the bottom of all the tea set pieces and trivet.

GARDEN LINE

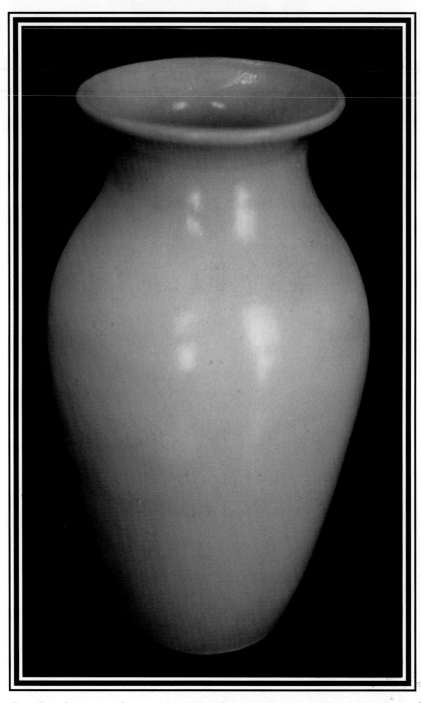

Garden line outdoor pot, 15", gloss white, marked Muncie,
$350.00 – 400.00.

RIGHT

Factory workers posing by large outdoor pot approximately 30", $500.00+.

LEFT

James Wilkins, foreman at Muncie Pottery Company, in his garden with a large garden pot in background.

STRAWBERRY AND FLOWER POTS

ROW 1

Shape #G1 - 5", hanging strawberry planter, matte green drip over rose, marked 5A, $150.00–175.00.

Shape #G3 - 4", smallest flower pot, matte green drip over pumpkin, marked Muncie-A, $100.00–125.00.

Shape #G1 - 5", hanging strawberry planter, odd gloss white over maroon, marked 3A, $150.00–175.00.

ROW 2

Shape #G2 - 6½", strawberry planter, black peachskin, marked 2A, $150.00–175.00.

Shape #G3 - 4", smallest flower pot, matte white drip over rose, unmarked, $100.00–125.00.

Shape #G2 - 6½", strawberry planter, matte white drip over blue, marked 5A, $150.00–175.00.

ROW 3

Shape #G5 - 7", largest flower pot, matte green drip over rose, marked 5A, $200.00–225.00.

Shape #G4 - 6", medium flower pot, matte green drip over pumpkin, marked A, $175.00–200.00.

Shape #G3 - 4", smallest flower pot, matte green drip over lilac, marked 5A, $100.00–125.00.

REUBEN HALEY DESIGNS
FIGURAL LINE, SPANISH LINE, AND ROMBIC LINE

FIGURAL LINE

ROW 1

Shape #434 - 12½", matte light green, "Lovebird" bowl, unmarked, rare, $700.00–800.00.

Shape #193 - 9", matte green drip over pumpkin, "Lovebird" vase, marked A3, $500.00–550.00.

ROW 2

Shape #434 - 12½", matte green drip over lilac, "Lovebird" bowl, unmarked rare, $700.00–800.00.

VASES (LEFT)

ROW 1

Shape #194 - 6½", matte green drip over rose, "Katydid" vase, marked 4, $300.00–350.00.
Shape #194 - 6½", orange peel, "Katydid" vase, marked Muncie-5A, $300.00–350.00.
Shape #194 - 6½", matte white drip over blue, "Katydid" vase, marked 5A, $300.00–350.00.

ROW 2

Shape #193 - 9", matte white drip over blue, "Lovebird" vase, marked 5A, $500.00–550.00.
Shape #189 - 9", matte green drip over lilac, "Goldfish" vase, marked 4, $450.00–500.00.

ROW 3

Shape #194 - 6½", matte blue drip over green, "Katydid" vase, marked 1A, $300.00–350.00.
Shape #193 - 9", gloss light green, "Lovebird" vase, marked 4, $500.00–550.00.

SPANISH LINE

ROW 1

Shape #278 - 5", gloss light blue, marked 4, $250.00–275.00.
Shape #275 - 6", matte green drip over rose, marked 5A, $300.00–350.00.
Shape #278 - 5", dark semi-gloss green, unmarked, $250.00–275.00.

ROW 2

Shape #277 - 4", matte green drip over green, marked 2A, $200.00–225.00 pair.
Shape #276 - 11", matte green drip over green, marked Muncie, $200.00–225.00.
Shape #277 - 4", matte green drip over green, marked 2A, $200.00–225.00 pair.

ROW 3

Shape #273 - 7", matte green drip over lilac, marked 1A, $225.00–250.00.
Shape #279 - 7", matte green drip over rose, marked 2A, $300.00–350.00.
Shape #273 - 7", gloss light blue, marked 4, $225.00–250.00.

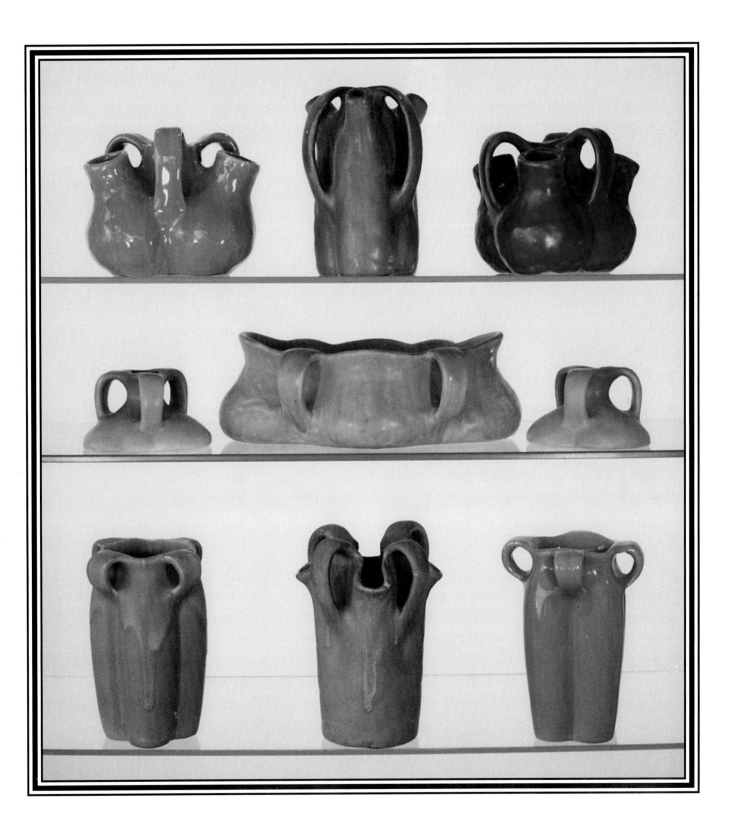

ROMBIC LINE

ROW 1

Shape #300 - 8", matte white drip over blue, marked A, $600.00 – 700.00.
Shape #309 - 7", matte blue airbrush over green, marked Muncie, $300.00 – 350.00.
Shape #307 - 7", matte green drip over rose, marked 2A, $800.00 – 1,000.00.
Shape #304 - 9", matte dark green, unmarked, $700.00 – 800.00.

ROW 2

Shape #308 - 6", matte green drip over rose, marked 2A, $500.00 – 550.00.
Shape #305 - 3", matte white drip over blue, marked Muncie-5A, $500.00 – 550.00 pair.
Shape #305 - 3", matte white drip over blue, marked 2A, $500.00 – 550.00 pair.
Shape #306 - 9", matte dark green, marked Muncie-A, $350.00 – 400.00.
Shape #301 - 6", matte green drip over pumpkin, marked 4, $500.00 – 550.00.

ROW 3

Shape #310 - 5", matte dark green, marked Muncie-A, $400.00 – 450.00.
Shape #302 - 4", matte green drip over rose, sugar bowl, unmarked, $400.00 – 450.00.
Shape #303 - 5", matte green drip over rose, creamer, unmarked, $300.00 – 350.00.
Shape #312 - 5", blue peachskin, marked A, $300.00 – 350.00.

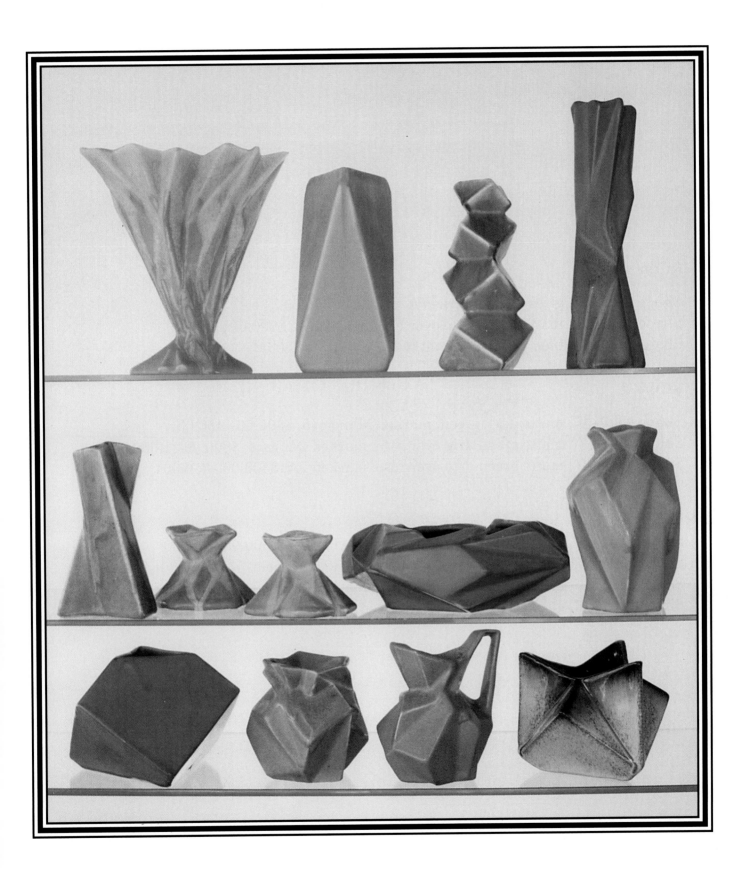

ROW 1

Shape #312 - 5", gloss black, marked A, $300.00–350.00.
Shape #300 - 8", matte white drip over blue, marked A, $600.00–700.00.
Shape #312 - 5", blue peachskin, marked A, $300.00–350.00.

ROW 2

Shape #310 - 5", matte dark green, marked Muncie-5, $400.00–450.00.
Shape #307 - 7", matte green drip over rose, marked 2A, rare, $800.00–1,000.00.
Shape #310 - 5", matte green drip over rose, marked 2A, $400.00–450.00.

ROW 3

Shape #301 - 6", matte green drip over rose, marked 2A, $500.00–550.00.
Shape #305 - 3", matte white drip over blue, marked Muncie-5A, $500.00–550.00 pair.
Shape #305 - 3", matte white drip over blue, marked 2A, $500.00–550.00 pair.
Shape #301 - 6", gloss medium green, marked A, $500.00–550.00.

LEFT

Shape #221 - 12", gloss blue drip over green, marked 1, rare, $1,000.00+.

RIGHT

Shape #220 - 10", matte green drip over rose, marked Muncie, $800.00 – 1,000.00.

Shape #220 - 8", gloss light blue, marked 1, $650.00 – 750.00.
Shape #220 - 6", matte dark green, marked 4, $550.00 – 600.00.
Shape #220 - 8", gloss light blue, marked 1, $650.00 – 750.00.

ROW 1

Shape #223 - 10", gloss black, marked Muncie, $700.00–800.00.
Shape #223 - 10", matte green drip over rose, marked 1, $700.00–800.00.

ROW 2

Shape #222 - 8½", gloss light green, unmarked, $350.00–400.00.
Shape #307L - 7", gloss black, marked Muncie-1, rare, $800.00–1,000.00.

LEFT

Shape #224 - 11", blue peachskin, marked 1K, $600.00 – 700.00.

RIGHT

Shape #224 - 11", blue peachskin, marked II, $600.00 – 700.00.

BOTTOM

Shade, not believed to be a factory original, looks homemade but looks great with the lamp.

Shape #U-45 - 5", matte green drip over rose, marked Muncie, $450.00–500.00.

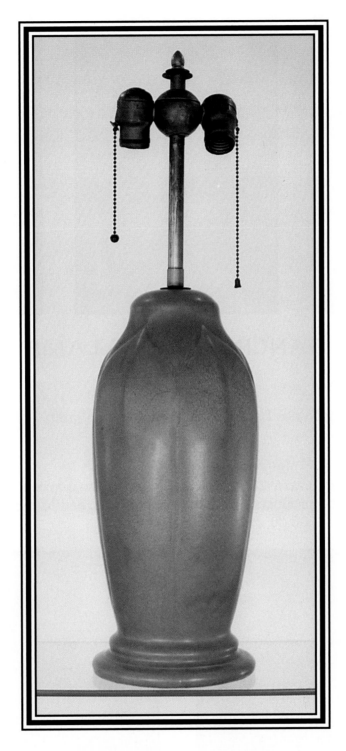

MUNCIE LAMPS

Shape #U32 - 15", matte green airbrush over rose, unmarked, $700.00–800.00. This is the largest Muncie Pottery lamp known. This lamp or its twin reportedly sat on Grafton's desk in his office at the Gill Clay Pot Company.

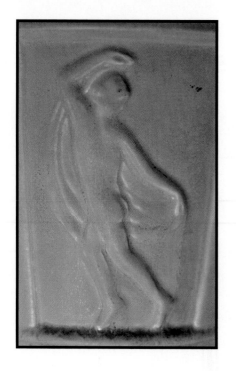
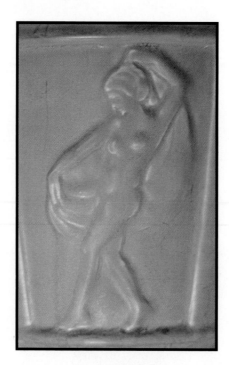

DANCING NUDES LAMP

ABOVE AND BELOW

Five panels of the Dancing Nudes Lamp, from a matte green lamp.

OPPOSITE PAGE

Shape #U33 - 10" (pottery part), 28½" overall height, matte green airbrush over pumpkin, (one of only two Muncie products featuring people), marked Muncie, $500.00–600.00 with original finial; $400.00–500.00 without finial.

ROW 1

Shape #240 - 12", light brown peachskin, marked 3, $275.00–300.00.
Shape #240 - 12", gloss green airbrush over white, marked 1E, $275.00–300.00.

ROW 2

Shape #236 - 6", blue peachskin, unmarked, $100.00–125.00.
Shape #236 - 6", gloss cobalt blue, marked 2D, $100.00–125.00.
Shape #236 - 6", matte green drip over rose, marked 1E, $100.00–125.00.
Shape #236 - 6", gloss black, marked 3, $100.00–125.00.
Shape #236 - 6", gloss creamy yellow with rust highlights on edges, marked 2, $100.00–125.00.

Shape #229 - 7", gloss black, marked 1M, $150.00–175.00.

Shape #229 - 7", gloss black, marked 3E, $150.00–175.00.

Shape #U34 - 10", gloss rust and cream blend, marked 2A, $275.00–300.00.

Shape #237 - 6", matte green airbrush over rose, unmarked, $125.00–150.00.

Shape #226 - 10", matte green drip over rose, marked 1E, $225.00 – 250.00.
Shape #226 - 12", matte green drip over rose, marked ??, $275.00 – 300.00.
Shape #226 - 10", black peachskin, unmarked, $225.00 – 250.00.

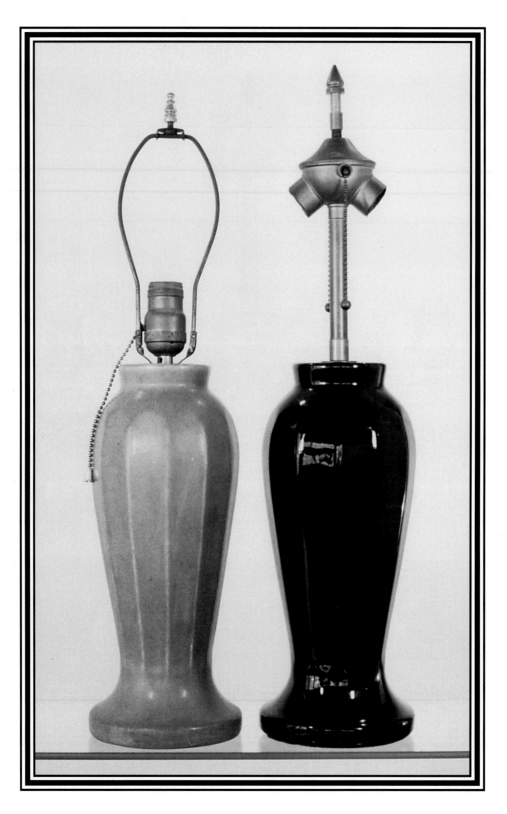

Shape #232 - 12½", matte blue airbrush over rose, marked 4, $275.00−300.00.
Shape #232 - 12½", gloss black, marked 1, $275.00−300.00.

Shape #143L - 7", matte blue airbrush over green, marked Muncie-5, $200.00–225.00.
Shape #144 - 12", matte rose, not a factory lamp, marked ??, $150.00–175.00.
Shape #143L - 7", matte white drip over blue, unmarked, $200.00–225.00.

Shape #U35 - 12" (pottery part), gloss cobalt drip over green, factory
lamp version of shape #144 - 12", marked 3, $275.00–300.00.

TOP

Shape #234 - 8", matte tri-color, unmarked, $150.00−175.00.

Shape #132 - 7", matte green drip over rose, unmarked, $175.00−200.00.

Shape #234 - 8", gloss mustard yellow, unmarked, $150.00−175.00.

RIGHT

Shape #234 - 10", matte blue over rose drip, marked B4, $250.00−275.00.

Shape #U36 - 12", gloss black, marked Muncie
Aladdin, $300.00–325.00.

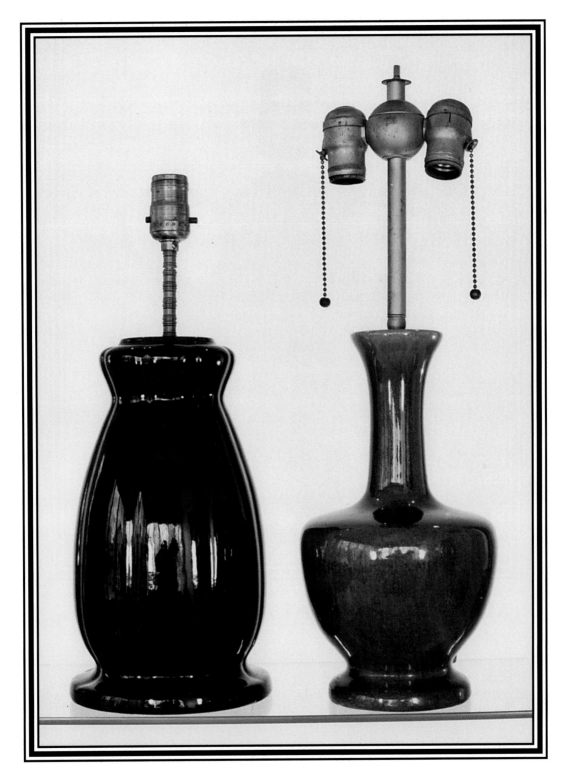

Shape #U37 - 12", gloss black, marked 4, (also has full Muncie Aladdin impression), $300.00–325.00.

Shape #U38 - 12", gloss mauve-brown, marked 2, $300.00–325.00.

MADE FOR THE ALADDIN MFG. CO.

ABOVE

Shape #U39 - 9", matte pumpkin (not a listed color for this lamp), unmarked, $200.00 – 225.00.

OPPOSITE PAGE

Shape #U39 - 9", matte white drip over blue (rare in this glaze, most are matte white drip over rose), unmarked, $250.00 – 275.00.

Shape #U39 - 9", matte white drip over rose (not pictured), $175.00 – 200.00.

TOP PHOTO

Shape #U40 - 8" lamp form of vase #181, matte green drip over pumpkin, unmarked, $200.00–225.00.

BOTTOM PHOTO

Shape #233 - 7", gloss maroon, marked IID, $150.00–175.00.
Shape #U41 - 9", matte green drip over lilac, unmarked, $250.00–275.00.
Shape #233 - 7", blue peachskin, marked 2B, $150.00–175.00.

Shape #244L - 10", blue peachskin,
marked B4, $200.00–225.00.

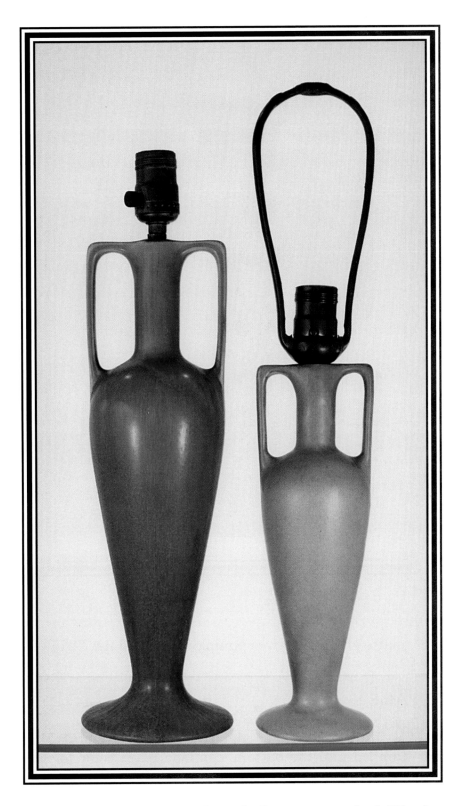

Shape #247 - 14", semi-gloss dark green, marked 3E, also
   has "247-14" molded into bottom, $300.00–350.00.

Shape #247 - 10", matte blue airbrush over rose, marked 4,
   $200.00–225.00.

ABOVE

Shape #U1 - 8", matte green drip over pumpkin, marked 2A, $275.00–300.00.

OPPOSITE PAGE

Shape #228 - 12", gloss mauve-brown, marked 3 and has the full Muncie Aladdin impression stamped into the bottom, common glaze color for this shape but rare elsewhere, $175.00–200.00.

Shape #228 - 12", gloss dark blue drip over green, marked 4 and has the full Muncie Aladdin impression stamped into the bottom, common glaze color, $175.00–200.00.

Shape #228 - 12", gloss cobalt blue, marked 4 and has the full Muncie Aladdin impression stamped into the bottom, rare glaze color, $175.00–200.00.

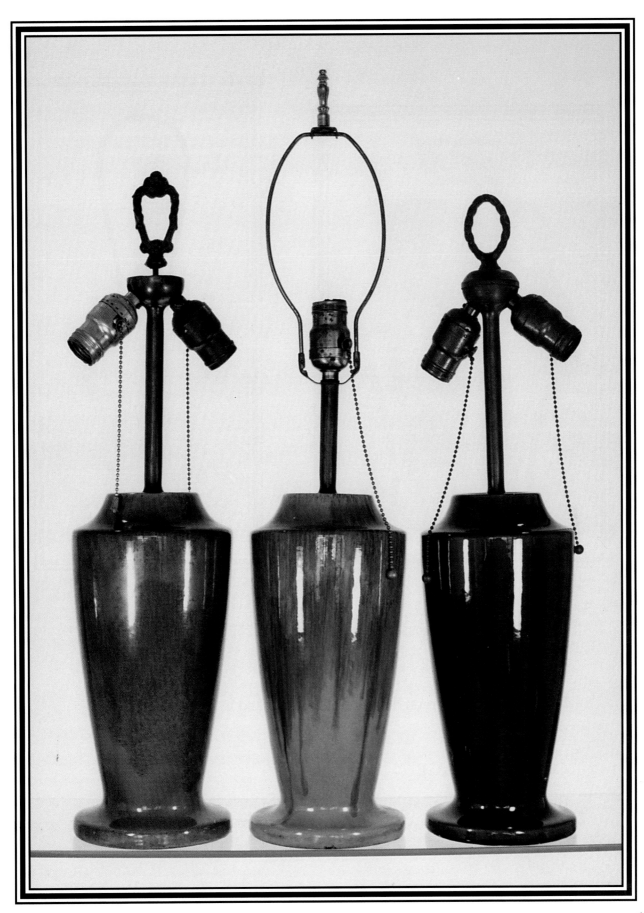

ABOVE LEFT

Shape #U42 - 10", gloss black unmarked, $225.00–250.00.

ABOVE RIGHT

Shape #U43 - 9", green drip over lilac, marked 4, $250.00–275.00.

OPPOSITE PAGE

Shape #246 - 12", gloss blue peachskin, unmarked, $275.00–300.00.

LEFT

Shape #U44 - 12", radio lamp, gloss rose on outside, gloss white interior, unmarked, $300.00–325.00.

RIGHT

Shape #U46 - 10", marked Muncie, $50.00 – 75.00 bisque; $250.00 – 275.00 glazed.

Similar to shape #422, handles added, unmarked.

TOP ROW

Left: Like shape #220 - 6", but the crispness of the mold makes one suspect, still a great looking lamp, unmarked.

Center: Bowl brought home from the factory by an employee, possibly while Arkansas potters were visiting. Glaze is not quite the same color as Muncie's green drip over pumpkin, unmarked.

Bottom: Loving cup has the look of Muncie's blue peachskin glaze, bottom could be correct but no proof since it is unmarked.

BOTTOM ROW

Left: Bowl purchased in Muncie, glaze color is correct but no proof of Muncie production since piece is unmarked.

Right: Flower frog, could be the frog for the larger version of shape #187 but no proof since it is unmarked.

LEFT

Pair of gloss black lamp bases purchased along with other pieces in the Muncie area. Bottom rim is slightly different from most Muncie lamp bases but it is close. Both are unmarked.

RIGHT

Gloss green over white vase is believed to actually be production Muncie but cannot be proved since vase is unmarked.

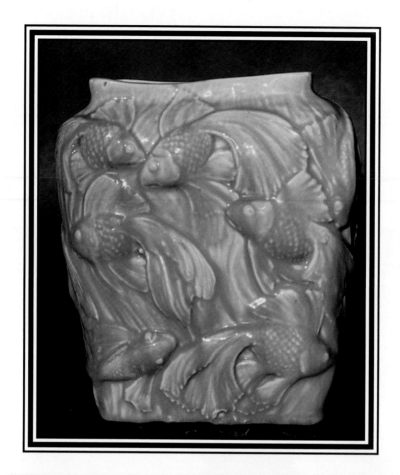

Beautifully molded and glazed goldfish vase was molded from a Muncie mold. However, it has markings from another potter incised into the bottom. This vase was probably made from a mold purchased from the factory dispersal sale around 1940.

THE WISCONSIN POTTERY

The English Wilkins family was involved in the ceramic arts across five generations, spanning more than 300 years. Their accumulated knowledge was passed from father to son in the traditional manner of the craft guild. James was superintendent of one of the old established potteries in Bristol when his son was born. William (Bill) W. Wilkins would join the family tradition at age 11 when he began his apprenticeship under the supervision of his father. William attended the Old College of Merchant Adventure located in Bristol and graduated in 1913 with a degree in ceramics technology.

The Wilkins family came to America in 1914, and from 1919 both James and William were instructors in Pottery Arts at the Lewis Institute in Chicago. In 1923, James came to Muncie to head the art pottery department for the Muncie Clay Products. William would stay at Lewis Institute until 1929. In the 1930s, William taught ceramics at the Fraternal Order of the Moose orphanage, Mooseheart, near Aurora, Illinois.

After the closure of the Muncie Potteries in 1939, James and William were offered half interest in the Wisconsin Pottery Company, a small pottery located in Pittsville, Wisconsin. The pottery was started by Father John Wilitzer, a Catholic priest, in 1931. Using local clay for their products, the Wis-Art designs were developed by the Wilkinses and many items resemble

William Wilkins hand throwing bowl on the wheel.

Muncie pottery designs although they are somewhat smaller. About 50 different shapes were marketed by the salesman/priest, Father Wilitzer, during its operation. Some of the pottery is unmarked; others are marked on the bottom with a hand-scribed number over and under a horizontal line. There are also two ink stamps, a two-line stamp (Pittsville Pottery - Wisconsin), and a three-line stamp (Pittsville - Pottery - Wis.) A diamond-shaped silver paper label with "Wisconsin Ceramics Pittsville Wisconsin" was used along with a rectangular Wis-Art decal. The pottery closed around 1943.

James Wilkins carrying sagger filled with vases on the way to the kiln.

The Wisconsin Pottery building, ca. 1939.

Father John Wilitzer.

Interior of the Wisconsin Pottery showing worker pouring slip into the molds. In the background is one of the kilns.

Green fluted 16" vase.

Small jar without top.

Pottery shown in this section are unmarked pieces that are attributed to both James and William Wilkins and are from the James Wilkins Estate.

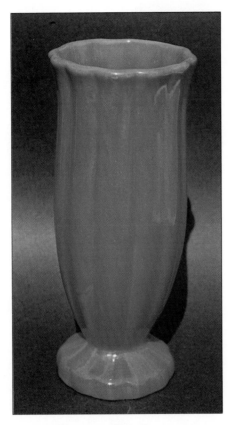

8" orange fluted vase.

12" peachskin urn.

Blue 6" fluted vase.

Silver diamond label.

3-piece console set.

Black two-handled lamp.

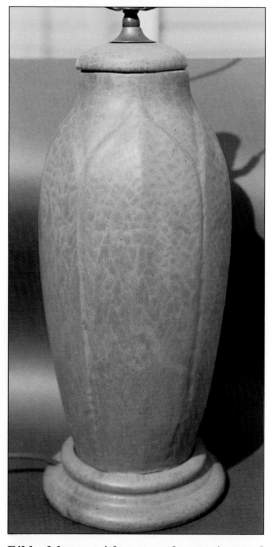

Ribbed lamp with unusual experimental glaze.

BOYS TOWN POTTERY

In 1940, William Wilkins was hired as instructor at Boys Town; with some assistance from his father James, he created and developed there what would become one of the best high school ceramic courses in the country. Thousands of boys were literally taught from the ground up with field trips to mine clay. Ancient methods along with modern production techniques were incorporated in the curriculum of the fine arts class and the five-year commercial pottery course. The exceptional caliber of workmanship and enthusiasm shown by the young student potters revealed itself in creations that rival the production pieces of the established Ohio potteries.

Over the years the pottery studio grew from its start in the old Recreation Building to its home in the Vocational Career Center, which was built in 1948 with modern facilities for all phases of the ceramic arts.

The popularity of the studio's wares was witnessed by the Boys Town Gift Shop where thousands of items were sold over the pottery's life span. The multitude of glazes was a product of James and William Wilkins' experimentation. James Wilkins died at Boys Town in 1950. William, who was head and heart of the Boys Town Pottery and mentor to all who knew him, followed his father in 1954. After William's death, the vitality of the pottery was never the same. Over the next three decades, interest in pottery declined, and the gift shop imported more and more souvenirs. The role the pottery had played in building boys into men was over. The pottery closed its doors in 1993.

Markings are inscribed on the bottom with "Boys Town" with a decal souvenir of Boys Town also used.

William Wilkins.

William Wilkins demonstrating the art of throwing for the Henry Fonda family.

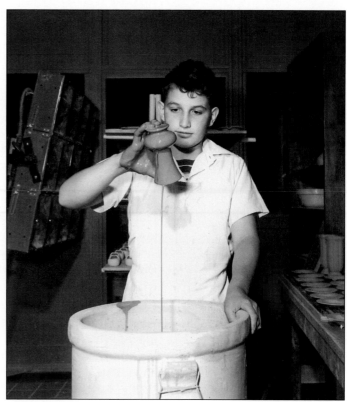

Scenes from the pottery classes at Boys Town, 1944.

Proud youthful potter and his creation.

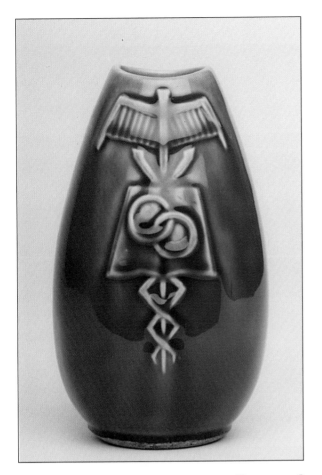

Items produced and sold at Boys Town.

Items produced and sold at Boys Town.

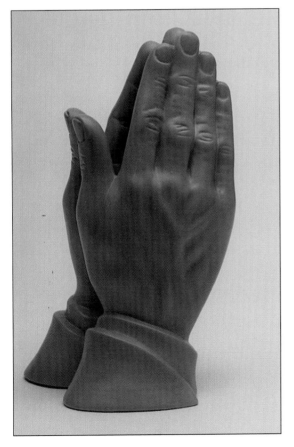

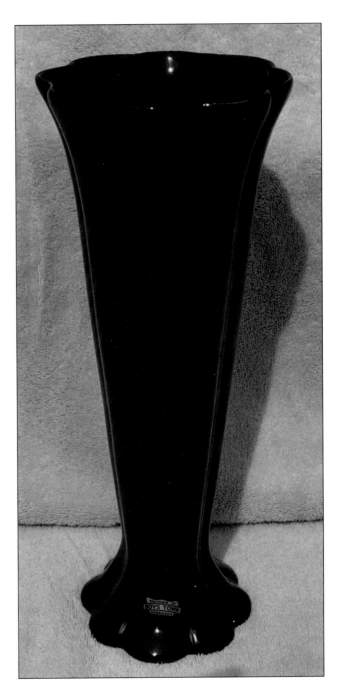

Items produced and sold at Boys Town.

ROW 1

Shoe, gloss white over green drip, marked "Boys Town."
Pelican, glass dark multi-color glaze, marked "Boys Town."
Shoe, gloss light blue, Wis-Art, marked "108/1-?1."
Vase, gloss lime green, Boys Town, marked "BT//."
Shoe, blue peachskin, marked "Boys Town."

ROW 2

Sugar with lid, gloss light blue, believed to be Wis-Art, identical to Muncie's except the Muncie version has an octagonal opening and this one has a round opening. Bottom of lid is also octagonal on the Muncie version, unmarked.

Vase, Wis-Art, gloss blue peachskin glaze, marked "WIS 402???"

Creamer, gloss light blue, believed to be Wis-Art, pouring spout has crease in the middle while the Muncie version is round, marked "PAT. 1925913."

ROW 3

Vase - 4½", gloss yellow, marked "WIS/102/11-1."

Canoe - 10", gloss brown, stamped on bottom "Compliments/Boernlein cheese factory," marked "5 1 5."

Vase - 4½", gloss white over blue, marked "boys town."

ALADDIN MANUFACTURING

Aladdin Manufacturing Company, makers of Aladdin Lamps of Muncie, was founded in 1919 by the flamboyant entrepreneur, Overton Sacksteder, Jr., with William Sacksteder as secretary/treasurer and G.M. Spencer as president. Incorporated in January 1925, Aladdin manufactured both metal and pottery lamps and became the largest consumer of Muncie pottery lamp bases, using a reported 8,000 pieces per week. Aladdin Manufacturing is sometimes confused with its rival, Aladdin Industries of Alexandria, Indiana, makers of Aladdin Kerosene Mantle Lamps and later Aladdin Electric Lamps.

Following the acquisition of Highlands Manufacturing in 1923, one of its suppliers of electrical fittings and manufacturers of metal floor and table lamps, Aladdin's sales skyrocketed from $5,000.00 its first year to $750,000 yearly by 1927. William Miller, a former Tiffany designer, joined the company that same year to produce a new line of lamps. In 1927, Aladdin also opened Household Electric, Inc., a retail store at 107 West Jackson Street to sell its products. R.D. Bache was in charge of this enterprise, and a complete line of Aladdin lamps and other electrical appliances were sold from this showroom. The R. Milt Retherford Manufacturing Company, Muncie's oldest lamp manufacturing company, was bought out of receivership by Aladdin in 1928. Aladdin used national advertising and a flying sales force to ensure the product's marketability throughout the United States. Excursions to South America, Europe, Australia, Cuba, and the Philippines by Aladdin officials introduced the "Aladdin Electric Portable Lamps" on a global scale.

The Aladdin Manufacturing Company was located at 18th and Hackley streets in the old Muncie incinerator building until it burned down in 1923. A new building was erected on the same site, next to Muncie's first airfield.

With the 1920s and 1930s national obsession with aviation, Overton Sacksteder, Jr., inventor of the gooseneck lamp, enlisted an acquaintance who owned a plane, which he christened the "Flying Showroom," which enabled him to travel widely to distributors in Chicago, Duluth, Milwaukee, Kansas City, and Grand Rapids. In his Flying Showroom, Sacksteder never failed to attract attention wherever he landed in the pursuit of new customers.

The relationship between the two Aladdin companies was amicable when

The Flying Showroom.

one firm produced kerosene lamps and the other electric lamps, but trouble began when the Alexandria firm started producing electric lamps with the name "Aladdin Portable Electric Lamps." Lawsuits were filed by Aladdin of Muncie, and years of litigation ensued. On November 11, 1935, the Supreme Court of the United States denied the appeal of the Muncie concern, resulting in the loss of their trade name to the Mantle Lamp Company of America, located in Chicago, the parent company of Alexandria's Aladdin Industries.

After years of litigation, the company was now in severe financial trouble. General Lamps was formed from the remains of the corporation and operated briefly at the Muncie site. In 1941, the company was moved to Elwood, Indiana, under the name Muncie Elwood Lamp Company. Metal lamps were manufactured only at this facility. After acquiring Fairies Lamp of Decatur, Illinois, in 1959, the company became Fairies-General Lamp. It was in turn bought out by Fostoria Glass of Fostoria, Ohio, in 1959.

Metal and pottery lamps being assembled in Aladdin factory.

Silk shades hand fitted to wire frames.

CATALOG REPRINTS

"HOW MUNCIE POTTERY IS MADE" PAMPHLET (1931)

This pamphlet dates from 1931 and was probably printed by A.E. Boyce Co. of Muncie, Indiana. Boyce also printed the company's stock certificates and catalogs.

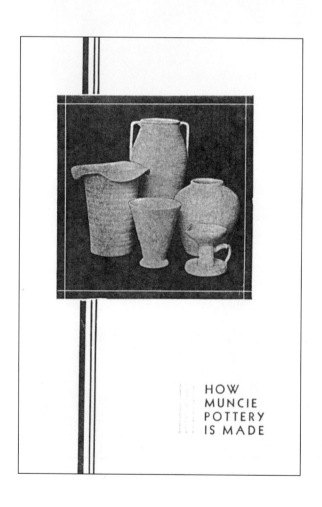

HOW
Muncie Pottery
IS MADE

THE ART of pottery making is as old as civilization itself. To trace its origin we must travel back over centuries of history, and then the date will elude us. Most races of the world felt a need for some sort of dish or bowl. Perhaps it was seeing a footprint harden in a sun-baked soil that first set them thinking they might fashion useful things of clay. Gradually this craft has come up through the ages, and been influenced by all races of people, each age and race adding its own characteristic touch. Pottery making, at the present time is a distinct art that gives to all the world objects of lasting beauty and practical value.

THE MUNCIE POTTERIES
MUNCIE, INDIANA

BLUNGING

THE first process in the manufacture of pottery is the preparation of the clay body. This consists in the blunging with water of the different clays, feldspar and flint for several hours, after which it is allowed to run over very fine screens where foreign articles of any nature are removed. It is then carried to the filter press where the water is squeezed out and the body is ready for the potter to turn on his wheel.

TURNING

THE origin of the potter's wheel is claimed by Greece, but later discoveries indicate that it was used in ages past by the Egyptians. One never tires of watching the potter manipulate the clay on the wheel. Until a few years ago, all pottery was made by turning the clay or by pressing it in the moulds. Today, however, the demand for more uniform products and greater quantities call for the use of the jigger wheel and the casting process.

MOULD MAKING

MAKING of models and plaster moulds is a very expensive operation and in many cases hundreds of dollars are expended before the first piece is taken from a mould. It is first necessary to turn the model, after which it is incased in plaster and the master mould is then made around the cast. From this master mould additional moulds are made and after several weeks drying they are ready for casting.

CASTING

IN the casting process the clay is not put through the filter press but is taken from the blungers and carefully screened through fine screens, after which it passes to the agitator where it is kept constantly in motion to prevent settling. The clay, about the consistency of thick cream, is poured in to the plaster moulds; the moulds being dry absorb the water from the clay. The desired thickness of the piece being cast is determined by the length of time the clay solution is allowed to stand in the mould. After the mould has absorbed the water from the clay to the proper thickness, it is inverted and that part of the clay from which the water has not been absorbed is allowed to run out, leaving a lining of clay about one-quarter inch in thickness adhering to the sides and bottom. This is allowed to remain in the mould until the next day, and the mould, being in several pieces, is then taken away from the piece of pottery which is now hard enough to handle and is sent to the finishing tables.

FINISHING

*E*ACH morning the finisher receives ware from the caster. The pieces are neatly trimmed and the ones cast in more than one section, such as pitchers and vases with handles, are carefully fitted together. The pottery is set aside until it becomes hard and dry, when it is again carefully gone over by the finishers using very fine sandpaper to remove any rough places, after which it is then sponged off with silk sponges, dried and sent to the kiln for firing.

FIRING

*A*LL our pottery is burnt twice; first in the bisque fire and then in the glost fire. The pieces to be burnt are placed in saggers, as shown in picture on the man's head. These saggers are made of very high-grade fire clay and are placed in the kiln one on top of the other to a height of approximately 12 feet. The bisque kiln will hold about 500 saggers and each sagger contains an average of 10 pieces of ware. The fire is then applied and the temperature is gradually raised until it reaches about 2500 degrees Fahrenheit, requiring approximately 48 hours. This high temperature is necessary to fuse the pottery body, which prevents the pottery from leaking. The kiln is then gradually cooled off and the ware, now hard and brittle, is sent to the glaze room for firing.

DIPPING

*E*ACH piece of pottery is submerged in a glaze solution. It is a very delicate operation, as the hardness of the piece determines the length of time it should be submerged. As the glaze is very costly, only operators of long experience are trusted with this work. Where the two-tone color effect is wanted, a different glaze is either sprayed over the first with air brushes, or that part of the piece requiring the different is submerged in another. The pieces are sent to the glost kiln where they are again placed in saggers and fired. Care is used in setting the ware on stilts in the saggers, and only a few pieces can be put in each sagger, as sufficient room must be left around each piece for the glaze to mature. Great care must be used in the firing of the glost kiln, as the variation of a few degrees of temperature will either over-fire or under-fire the pottery. When the proper temperature is reached the kiln is tightly sealed and is gradually cooled to a temperature that will admit handling of the finished pottery.

THE MUNCIE POTTERIES

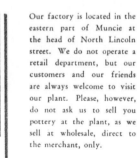

Our factory is located in the eastern part of Muncie at the head of North Lincoln street. We do not operate a retail department, but our customers and our friends are always welcome to visit our plant. Please, however, do not ask us to sell you pottery at the plant, as we sell at wholesale, direct to the merchant, only.

THE MUNCIE POTTERIES
MUNCIE, INDIANA

W. ARTHUR SWIFT PHOTOGRAPHS

W. Arthur Swift, born on October 6, 1888, came to Muncie in 1918, taking a position with the Delaware Engraving Company as one of Muncie's early commercial photographers documenting life in Muncie during the 1920s. Swift took the following photos on February 10, 1924. These represent some of the first examples of the "Artistic Pottery" designs. It appears that a good many of the shapes were discontinued, although some appeared in the 1926 catalog. Examples of the deleted designs are quite rare. The original photos show some amount of retouching by Swift, and it is possible these were test photos for a proposed catalog or perhaps a salesman's sample portfolio.

Advertisement from Muncie City Directory.

229-7"

236-6"

132-7½"

237-6"

234-7"

233-7"

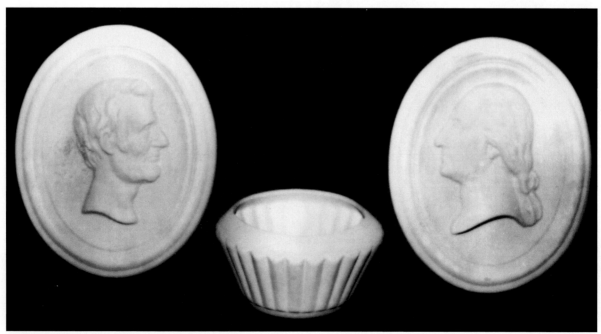

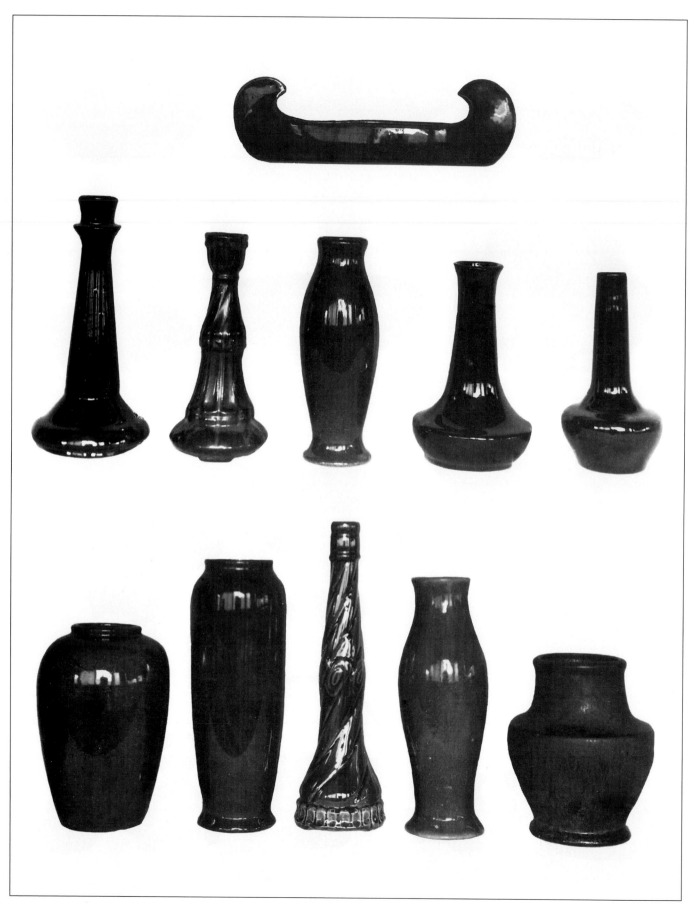

Round kiln with Maxon burner, ca. 1929.

ALADDIN LAMPS, CATALOG NO. 26

In the following Aladdin catalogs, only the pottery lamp sections are represented.

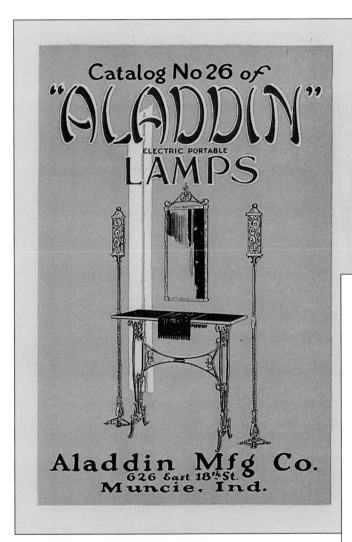

"ALADDIN" LAMPS

"ALADDIN" POTTERY END TABLE LAMPS

HEIGHT OF STAND 21"   LIST $7.50 EACH   DIAMETER OF SHADE 9"

STANDARD PACKAGE ANY SIX

NO. 311/721
BLUE MAT

*† NO. 312/722
BLACK GLAZE

NO. 313/723
BLUE OVER ROSE

SET No. 9304—6 Assorted (Two each as shown above) weight 35 lbs., LIST $45.00

Hand painted Parchment shades only List $2.00 each.

Genuine pottery base stands wired List $5.50 each.

These lamps are equipped with 8' (underwriters approved) silk cord, 2-piece plugs and push sockets.

"ALADDIN" BED LAMPS COMPLETE

HEIGHT 7"   LIST $5.00 EACH   WIDTH 8"

STANDARD PACKAGE ANY TWELVE

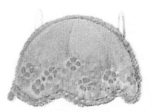

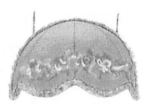

NO. 950
BLUE

*† NO. 951
PINK

NO. 952
GOLD

SET No. 9980—12 Assorted (Four each as shown above) weight 25 lbs., LIST $60.00

Hand Painted Beaded Cloth Shades only, without sockets, cords or plugs, List $4.00 each.

These lamps are equipped with 9' (underwriters approved) silk cord, 2-piece plugs and pull chain sockets.

---

* Can furnish 133 line screen halftone.   † Can furnish newspaper cuts.   Page Thirteen

"ALADDIN" LAMPS

"ALADDIN" COLONIAL OIL LAMPS

HEIGHT OF STAND 22½"   LIST $15.00 EACH   DIAMETER OF SHADE 17"

STANDARD PACKAGE ANY SIX

NO. 304/701

HUNTING SCENE

Shades are of parchment with antique applique of a steel engraving.

STAND is a replica of the old colonial oil lamp.

*† NO. 304/703
CRYSTAL BASE

NO. 304/702

FASHION PLATE

These lamps can be furnished with shades as shown in Set No. 9834 on page 19. For this combination use Set No. 9302, for two-lite at List $14.25 each or No. 9301 for one-lite at List $12.25 each.

SET No. 9307—6 Assorted (Two each as described above) weight 37 lbs., LIST $90.00

Parchment shades only List $9.00 each.
Crystal two light stands wired List $6.00 each.
Crystal one light stands wired List $4.00 each.
These lamps are equipped with 8' (underwriters approved) silk cord, 2-piece plugs and two pull chain sockets.

"ALADDIN" LUSTER BASE TABLE LAMPS

HEIGHT OF STAND 22"   LIST $15.00 EACH   DIAMETER OF SHADE 17"

STANDARD PACKAGE ANY SIX

*† NO. 8041
BLACK

NO. 8042
MULBERRY AND BLUE

* NO. 8043
DARK BLUE

SET No. 8040—6 Assorted (Two each as shown above) weight 52 lbs., LIST $90.00

Hand painted beaded parchment shades only List $8.25 each.
Luster, cast metal mounted two light, stands List $6.75 each.

These lamps are equipped with 8' (underwriters approved) silk cord, 2-piece plugs and two pull chain sockets.

Page Sixteen   * Can furnish 133 line screen halftone.   † Can furnish newspaper cuts.

207

"ALADDIN" LAMPS

"ALADDIN" LUSTER BASE TABLE LAMPS

HEIGHT OF STAND 22"   LIST $15.00 EACH   LENGTH OF SHADE 17½"

STANDARD PACKAGE OF SIX

| NO. 815/715 | NO. 816/716 | NO. 817/717 |
| CHERRY AND BLACK | YELLOW ROSE AND BLACK | VINE AND BLACK |

SET No. 9305—6 Assorted (Two each as shown above) weight 50 lbs., LIST $90.00

Hand painted beaded cloth shades only List $8.00 each.
Hand painted luster, cast metal mounted two light, stands wired List $7.00 each.

These lamps are equipped with 8' (underwriters approved) silk cord, 2-piece plugs and two pull chain sockets.

"ALADDIN" LUSTER BASE TABLE LAMPS

HEIGHT OF STAND 22"   LIST $15.00 EACH   LENGTH OF SHADE 17½"

STANDARD PACKAGE ANY SIX

| NO. 8081 | NO. 8082 | * NO. 8083 |
| WITH BLACK SHADE | WITH BLUE SHADE | WITH TAN SHADE |

SET No 8080—6 Assorted (Two each, as shown above) weight 52 lbs., LIST $90.00

Beaded cretonne shade only List $8.25 each.
Luster, cast metal mounted two light, stands wired List $6.75 each.

These lamps are equipped with 8' (underwriters approved) silk cord, 2-piece plugs and two pull chain sockets.

* Can furnish 133 line screen halftone.   † Can furnish newspaper cuts.   Page Seventeen

"ALADDIN" LAMPS

"ALADDIN" LUSTER BASE BOUDOIR LAMPS

HEIGHT OF STAND 12½"   LIST $5.50 EACH   LENGTH OF SHADE 7½"

STANDARD PACKAGE ANY TWELVE

NO. 283/610   *† NO. 285/611   NO. 284/612
APPLE GREEN SHADE   ORCHID SHADE   LAVENDER SHADE

SET No. 9202—12 Assorted (Four each as shown above) weight 30 lbs., LIST $66.00

Georgette shades only List $3.00 each.
Luster, cast metal mounted stands, wired List $2.50 each.

These lamps are equipped with 6' (underwriters approved) silk cord, 2-piece plugs and push sockets.

"ALADDIN" DRESDEN CHINA BOUDOIR LAMPS

HEIGHT OF STAND 13"   LIST $6.00 EACH   LENGTH OF SHADE 7½"

STANDARD PACKAGE ANY TWELVE

NO. 205/611   NO. 207/610   * NO. 209/612

WITH   WITH   WITH
ORCHID   GREEN   LAVENDER
GEORGETTE   GEORGETTE   GEORGETTE
SHADE   SHADE   SHADE

NO. 204/611   NO. 206/610   NO. 208/612

SET No. 9209—12 Assorted (Two each as shown above) weight 40 lbs., LIST $72.00

Georgette Shades only List $3.00 each.
Dresden Stands only List $3.00 each.

"ALADDIN" LAMPS

"ALADDIN" LUSTER BASE GEORGETTE SHADE TABLE LAMPS

HEIGHT OF STAND 22"   LIST **$17.50** EACH   OBLONG SHADE 21" LONG

STANDARD PACKAGE ANY SIX

NO. 8035
WITH BLUE SHADE

*† NO. 8034
WITH GOLD SHADE

NO. 8033
WITH ROSE SHADE

SET No. 8032—6 Assorted (Two each as shown above) weight 60 lbs., LIST **$105.00**
Oblong Silk Shades (Covered with Georgette) only List **$10.75** each.
Luster, cast metal mounted two light, stands wired List **$6.75** each.
These lamps are equipped with 8' (underwriters approved) silk cord, 2-piece plugs and two pull chain sockets.

———— ✄ ————

HEIGHT OF STAND 22"   LIST **$15.00** EACH   LENGTH OF SHADE 18"

STANDARD PACKAGE ANY SIX

NO. 8171
CHERRY AND BLACK

NO. 8173
YELLOW ROSE AND BLACK

NO. 8172
VINE AND BLACK

SET No. 8170—6 Assorted (Two each as shown above) weight 50 lbs., LIST **$90.00**
Oblong silk shade (covered with georgette) only List **$8.00** each.

Hand painted luster, cast metal mounted two light, stands wired List **$7.00** each.

These lamps are equipped with 8' (underwriters approved) silk cord, 2-piece plugs and two pull chain sockets.

Page Eighteen   * Can furnish 133 line screen halftone.   † Can furnish newspaper cuts.

"ALADDIN" ONE LIGHT LUSTER BASE TABLE LAMPS

HEIGHT OF STAND 20"   LIST **$12.25** EACH 1 LIGHT   DIAMETER OF SHADE 18"

STANDARD PACKAGE ANY SIX

| NO. 8073 | NO. 8072 | NO. 8074 |
| BLUE | BLACK | ROSE |

SET No. 8071—6 Assorted (Two each as shown above) weight 50 lbs., LIST $73.50

Silk shades only, List **$8.00** each.
Luster, cast metal mounted one light, stands wired List **$4.25** each.

These lamps are equipped with 8' (underwriters approved) silk cord, 2-piece plugs and two pull chain sockets.

——— ✄ ———

HEIGHT OF STAND 22"   LIST **$12.25** EACH 1 LIGHT   DIAMETER OF SHADE 18"

STANDARD PACKAGE ANY SIX

| NO. 8091 | NO. 8092 | * NO. 8093 |
| BLUE | ROSE | BLACK |

SET No. 8090—6 Assorted (Two each as shown above) weight 60 lbs., LIST $73.50

Hand painted beaded cloth shades only List **$8.00** each.
Luster, cast metal mounted one light, stands wired List **$4.25** each.

These lamps are equipped with 8' (underwriters approved) silk cord, 2-piece plugs and two pull chain sockets.

* Can furnish 133 line screen halftone.   † Can furnish newspaper cuts.   Page Nineteen

ALADDIN LAMPS, CATALOG NO. 29

Early photo of the Aladdin plant.

22

"ALADDIN" LAMPS

"ALADDIN" MODERN TABLE LAMPS
STANDARD PACKAGE—ANY THREE

No. 1334/1733
BLUE CRINKLED
LIST, $17.50

Shade No. 1733 is Gold Georgette Pleated with Green Alanoid Panel, China Silk Lining.

Shade No. 1732 is Sand Georgette Pleated with Amber Alanoid Panel, China Silk Lining.

Shade No. 1734 is Brown Ombre Georgette Pleated with Amber Alanoid Panel, China Silk Lining.

Shades, Size 9½ x 15"

LIST, Shades Only, $12.50 EACH

No. 1332/1732
LAVENDER BRONZE
CRINKLED
LIST, $17.50

No. 1333/1734
BLACK CRINKLED
LIST, $17.50

Stands, Height of Stand, 22".
LIST, Stands Only, $5.00 EACH

SET No. 9379—3 Assorted [1 Each as Shown Above] List, $52.50 for 3
Shipping Weight, 32 Lbs.

23

"ALADDIN" TABLE LAMPS
STANDARD PACKAGE—ANY SIX

Shades are Hand-Painted Parchment, with Black Velvet Binding. Size 9 x 17"

LIST, Shades Only, $2.50 EACH

No. 336/813
Black with Embossed
Bird Decoration
LIST, $7.50

No. 336/812
Black with Embossed
Bird Decoration
LIST, $7.50

Stand, Two-Light. Height, 20".
LIST, Stands Only, $5.00 EACH

No. 336/811
Black with Embossed
Bird Decoration
LIST, $7.50

SET No. 9328—6 Assorted [2 Each as Shown Above] List, $45.00 for 6
Shipping Weight, 43 Lbs.

36

"ALADDIN" LAMPS

"ALADDIN" BOUDOIR LAMPS

Stand, 12" High. LIST, $2.00 EACH.   Shades, Diameter 7". LIST, $2.50.

STANDARD PACKAGE—ANY TWELVE

LIST, $4.50 EACH

283/610	285/611	284/612
BLACK	ROSE	BLUE
Green Georgette Shade	Coral Georgette Shade	Orchid Georgette Shade

STANDS ARE LUSTER WITH CAST METAL MOUNTING

SET No. 9202—12 Assorted [4 Each as Shown Above] List, $48.00 for 12
Shipping Weight, 30 Lbs.

Stand, 12" High. LIST, $2.00 EACH.   Shade, Diameter 8", LIST, $2.00. EACH.

STANDARD PACKAGE—ANY TWELVE

LIST, $4.00 EACH

| 283/685 | 284/684 | 285/683 |
| BLACK | BLUE | ROSE |

SHADES ARE HAND-PAINTED PARCHMENT

STANDS ARE LUSTER WITH CAST METAL MOUNTING

SET No. 9203—12 Assorted [4 Each as Shown Above] List, $48.00 for 12
Shipping Weight, 30 Lbs.

"ALADDIN" POTTERY END TABLE LAMPS

STANDARD PACKAGE—ANY SIX

Shade No. 730 Orchid Georgette Pleated over Lavender Silk Mull.

Shade No. 732 Coral Georgette Pleated over Gold Silk Mull.

Shade No. 731 Green Georgette Pleated over Peach Mull.

Size 8 x 8 x 12"

LIST. Shades Only, $5.00 EACH.

No. 311/730
BLUE MATT
LIST, $10.00 EACH

No. 313/732
ROSE MATT
LIST, $10.00 EACH

No. 312/731
BLACK GLAZE
LIST, $10.00 EACH

Stands are One Light. Genuine Pottery.

Height, 20"

LIST Stands Only, $5.00 EACH.

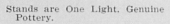

SET No. 9311—6 Assorted [Two Each as Shown Above] List, $60.00 for 3
Shipping Weight, 40 Lbs.

30

"ALADDIN" LAMPS

"ALADDIN" END TABLE LAMPS
STANDARD PACKAGE—ANY SIX

Shades are Hand-Painted, Beaded, with Black Velvet Binding. Size, 8 x 9".

LIST, Shades Only, $2.50 EACH

No. 312/722
BLACK
GLAZE
LIST, $7.50

No. 313/723
ROSE MATT
LIST, $7.50

No. 311/721
BLUE MATT
LIST, $7.50

Stands are One Light.   Height, 20"
LIST, Stands Only, $5.00 EACH

SET No. 9304—6 Assorted [2 Each as Shown Above] List, $45.00 for 6
Shipping Weight, 45 Lbs.

ALADDIN LAMPS, CATALOG NO. 33

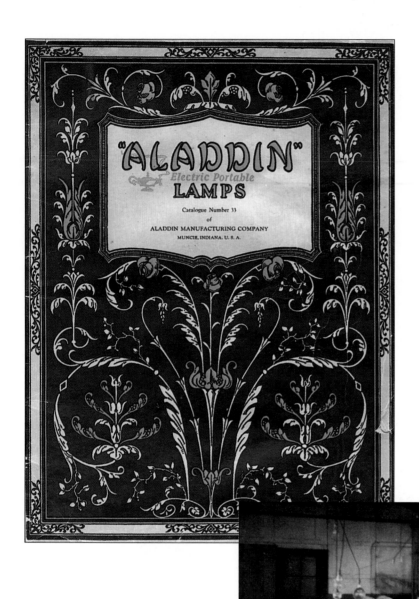

Skilled workers reverse painting glass shades at Aladdin, ca. 1925.

12   **"ALADDIN"** **LAMPS**

"ALADDIN" GLAZED POTTERY COLUMN TABLE LAMPS WITH LITHOGRAPHED AND RIBBON DECORATED PARCHMENT SHADES
LIST $5.00 EACH

443/1103
LAMP COMPLETE
List, $5.00 Each

No. 443
Stand Only
Colonial Gold and Green
List, $4.00 Each

No. 1103
Shade Only
Gold Border, Applique Print
Parchment
List, $1.00 Each
Stand 25" high; Shade 16"

444/2784
LAMP COMPLETE
List, $5.00 Each

No. 444
Stand Only
Colonial Gold and Wine
List, $4.00 Each

No. 2784
Shade Only
Early American in Brown
Tones Parchment.
List, $1.00 Each
Stand 25" high; Shade 16"

445/1102
LAMP COMPLETE
List, $5.00 Each

No. 445
Stand Only
Colonial Gold and Canary
List, $4.00 Each

No. 1102
Shade Only
Poinsetta Gold Applique
Print Parchment
List, $1.00 Each
Stand 25" high; Shade 16"

440/1107
LAMP COMPLETE
List, $5.00 Each

No. 440
Stand Only
Colonial Gold and Wine
List, $3.50 Each

No. 1107
Shade Only
Clear Parchment Laced with
Wine Colored Satin Ribbon
List, $1.50 Each
Wrapped in Cellophane
Stand 21" high; Shade 14"

441/1108
LAMP COMPLETE
List, $5.00 Each

No. 441
Stand Only
Colonial Gold and Green
List, $3.50 Each

No. 1108
Shade Only
Clear Parchment Laced With
Green Colored Satin Ribbon
List, $1.50 Each
Wrapped in Cellophane
Stand 21" high; Shade 14"

442/1109
LAMP COMPLETE
List, $5.00 Each

No. 442
Stand Only
Colonial Gold and Cream
List, $3.50 Each

No. 1109
Shade Only
Clear Parchment Laced With
Cream Colored Satin Ribbon
List, $1.50 Each
Wrapped in Cellophane
Stand 21" high; Shade 14"

SET No. 9377—6 assorted (one each as shown above) LIST $30.00 for 6 Complete.
Shipping Weight, 45 Lbs. Approximately

Note: Any of these lamps can be furnished with any of the designs of parchment shades shown on page 22, and to arrive at List complete simply add to the List of the stand only as indicated above, the list on page 22 of the shade selected.

30

"ALADDIN" LAMPS

"ALADDIN" "TWO-TONE" POTTERY 1-LIGHT TABLE LAMPS WITH LITHOGRAPHED PARCHMENT SHADES

Standard Package—Any Six

Stands Only, Height 19" to 21"; LIST, $3.00 EACH   LIST, $4.00 EACH COMPLETE   Shades Only, 18" Diam., LIST, $1.00 EACH

No. 372/2789
White over Blue Stand
with Yellow and Black
18" Parchment Shade

No. 373/2791
Green Over Rose Stand
with Deep Asters
18" Parchment Shade

No. 381/2732
White Over Rose Stand
With Tinted Rose Scene
Women in Garden
18" Parchment Shade

THIS "TWO-TONE" POTTERY IS BEAUTIFUL

No. 374/2790
Blue over Green Stand
with Brown Tones
18" Parchment Shade

No. 382/2788
Green over Lilac Stand
with Rose Design
18" Parchment Shade

No. 383/2733
Green over Orange Stand
with Berries in a Bowl Design
Tinted Apple Green
18" Parchment Shade

SET No. 7225—6 assorted (one each as shown above) LIST, $24.00 for 6.

Shipping Weight, 48 Lbs.

MUNCIE ARTISTIC POTTERY CATALOG

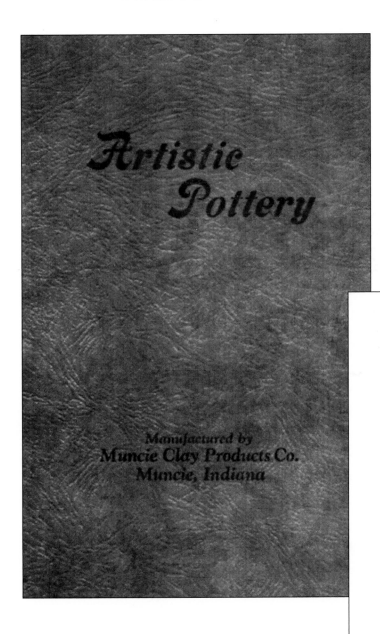

Our assortments are made up of the best selling articles and our latest designs are included in assortments.

$100.00 ASSORTMENT

77 Pieces. 46 Different Designs in Assorted Colors
Listed in Catalogue at $104.85
Price of Assortment $100.00

$200.00 ASSORTMENT

174 Pieces. 74 Designs in Assorted Colors
Makes a very attractive display
Listed in Catalogue at $210.50
Price of Assortment $200.00

If Assortments are desired in Mat Colors,
add 10% to above prices

Color List of Pottery

BRIGHT GLAZES

Black	Ivory	Dark Blue
Green	Yellow	Light Blue

Two-Color Bright Glaze Combination

Green drip over Ivory
Blue drip over Green

Three-Color Bright Glaze Combination

Black, Red, Yellow

MAT GLAZES

Add 10% to Catalogue Prices for Mat Glazes
ROSE   BLUE   GREEN

Two-Color Mat Glaze Combination

Blue drip on Rose
Green drip on Rose

Our line consists of artistic shapes, finished in attractive glazes that appeal to the average customer who is looking for something good at a reasonable price.

All items are listed as per dozen pieces

TERMS 2% 10 days, 30 days net.
All shipments F. O. B. Muncie, Ind.

No Packing Charges on orders of $20.00 net or more 25 cents per carton for packing smaller orders

MUNCIE CLAY PRODUCTS CO.
MUNCIE, INDIANA

ARTISTIC POTTERY

No. 196

No. 185
12 in., Bowl, $30.00
7 in., Bowl, $12.00

No. 196
4 in., Candle Stick
$6.00

No. 186
8 in., Vase, $30.00

No. 195

No. 183
11 in., Bowl, $36.00

No. 195
9 in., Candle Stick, $18.00

Muncie Clay Products Co., Muncie, Indiana

ARTISTIC POTTERY

No. 107
6 in.. $7.20

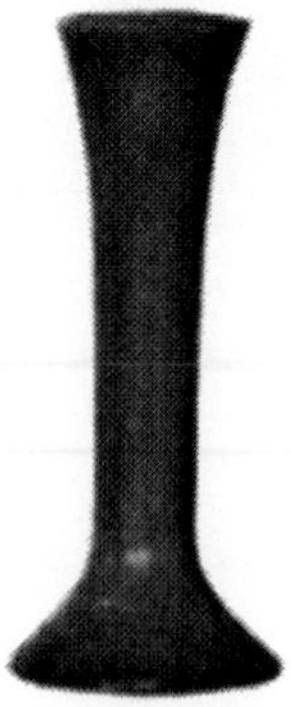

No. 109
6 in.. $7.20

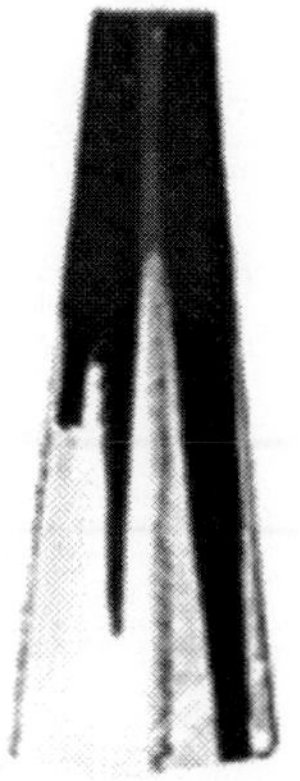

No. 108
6 in.. $7.20

No. 100
6 in.. $ 7.20
8 in.. 12.00
10 in.. 18.00
12 in.. 36.00
20 in . 180.00

No. 269
Cigarette Holder. $7.20
With Base Attached
$12.00

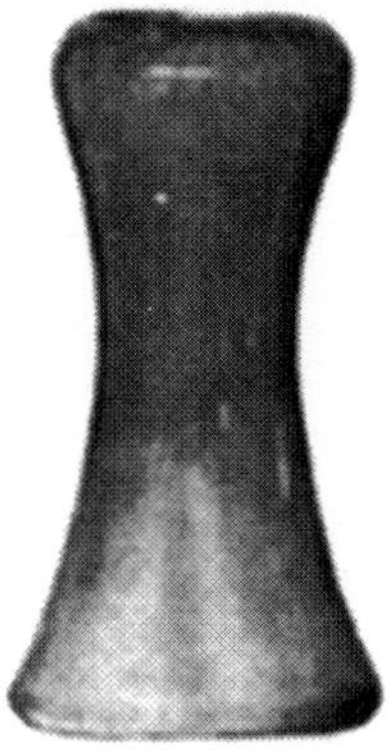

No. 119
6 in.. $7.20

No. 270
$12.00 per doz. sets

Muncie Clay Products Co.. Muncie, Indiana

ARTISTIC POTTERY

No. 104
8 in., $9.00

No. 112
8 in., $12.00

No. 225
A — 8 in., $15.00
B — 10 in. 24.00

No. 119
9 in., $18.00
12 in., 36.00

No. 261
9 in., $18.00

No. 259
9 in., $18.00

No. 105
6 in., $9.00

No. 106
7 in., $9.00

No. 115
6 in., $15.00

No. 102
A — 5 in . $ 9.00
B — 7 in., 18.00
C — 9 in.. 30.00

Muncie Clay Products Co., Muncie, Indiana

ARTISTIC POTTERY

No. 101
12 in., $36.00

No. 238
5 in., $ 9.00
9 in.,   24.00

No. 215
12 in., $36.00

No. 121
12 in., $48.00

No. 122
12 in., $35.00

No. 123
12 in., $42.00
No. 124 is No. 123 Ribbed
12 in., $42.00

No. 126
12 in., $48.00

No. 130
12 in., $48.00

No. 272
8 in., $10.80

Muncie Clay Products Co., Muncie, Indiana

ARTISTIC POTTERY

No. 128
12 in., $42.00

No. 129
11 in., $48.00

No. 136
12 in., $36.00

No. 137
11 in., $36.00

No. 144
A — 6½ in., $12.00
B — 8½ in., 18.00
C — 12 in., 36.00

No. 176
8 in., $36.00

No. 120
10 in., $15.00

No. 266
9 in., $18.00
Wall Pocket

No. 134
A — 7 in., $15.00
B — 10 in., 30.00

Muncie Clay Products Co., Muncie, Indiana

ARTISTIC POTTERY

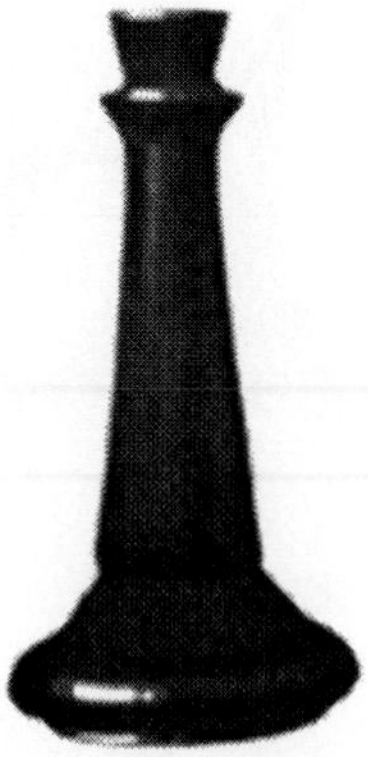

No. 150
9½ in., $12.00

No. 173
8 in., $36.00

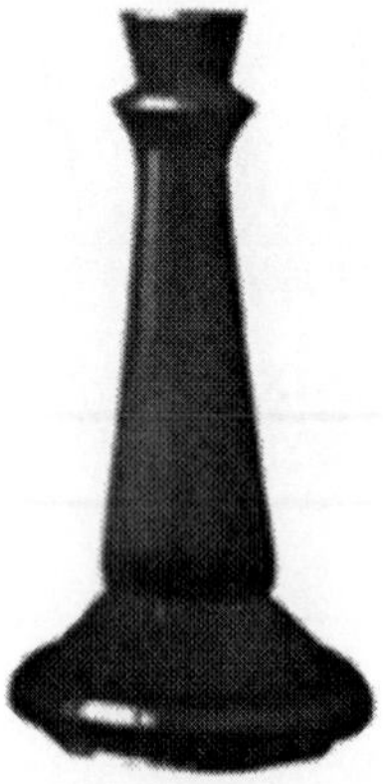

No. 150
9½ in., $12.00

No. 154
9 in., $18.00

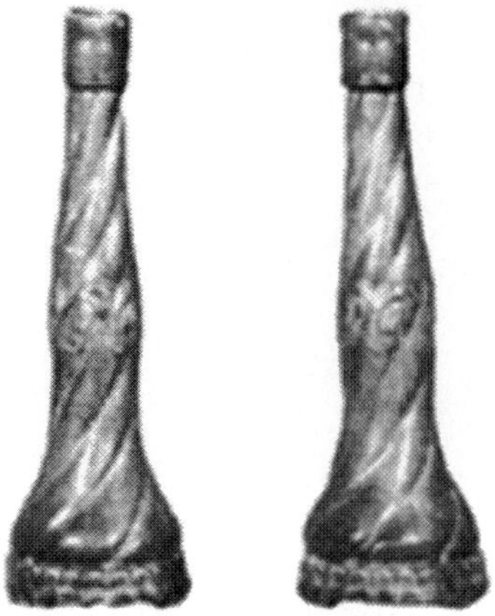

No. 155
13 in., $30.00

No. 152
4 in., $12.00

No. 153
4½ in., $9.00

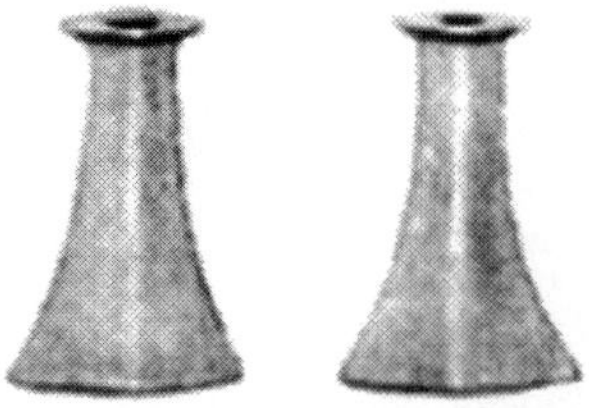

No. 149
6 in., $7.20

No. 211
7½ in., $24.00

No. 170
5 in., $9.00

No. 212
5 in., $9.00

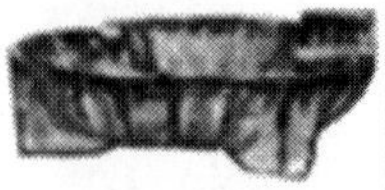

No. 213
5½ in., $12.00

Muncie Clay Products Co., Muncie, Indiana

ARTISTIC POTTERY

No. 265
7½ in., $24.00

No. 110
3½ in., $7.20

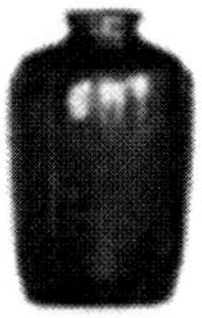

No. 111
5 in., $7.20

No. 113
4 in., $7.20

No. 206
4 in., $4.20

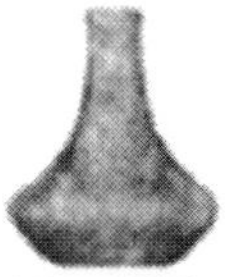

No. 116
3½ in., $7.20

No. 117
3½ in., $7.20

No. 118
3½ in., $7.20

No. 145
4 in., $9.00

No. 162
8 in., $24.00

No. 163
7 in., $21.00

No. 258
7 in., $24.00

No. 164
6 in., $18.00

No. 157
11 in., $36.00

No. 158
12 in., $36.00

No. 159
11 in., $48.00

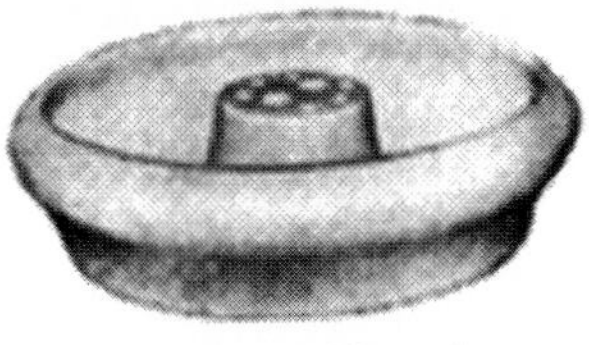

No. 164 — Nut Bowl
8 in., $24.00

No. 167
10 in., $36.00

Muncie Clay Products Co., Muncie, Indiana

A R T I S T I C   P O T T E R Y

No. 165
8½ in., $24.00

No. 166
7 in., $18.00

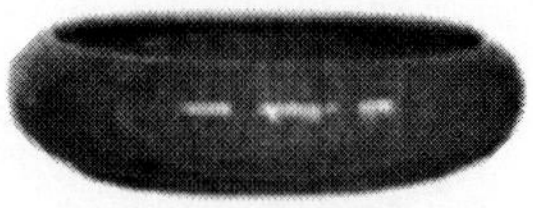

No. 168
5   in., $ 6.00
6½ in.,   7.20
8½ in.,   12.00

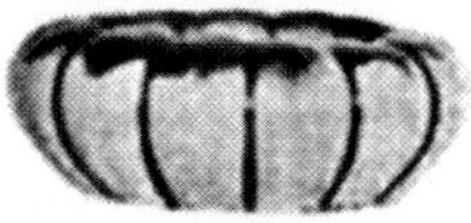

No. 169
7 in., $18.00
9 in.,   30.00

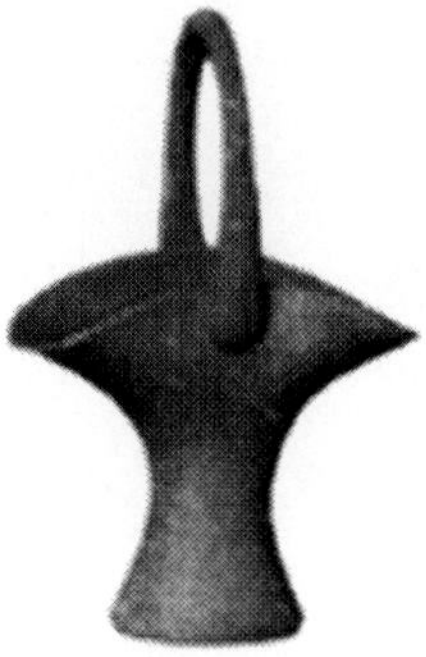

No 174
12 in., $30.00

No. 177
7 in., $36.00

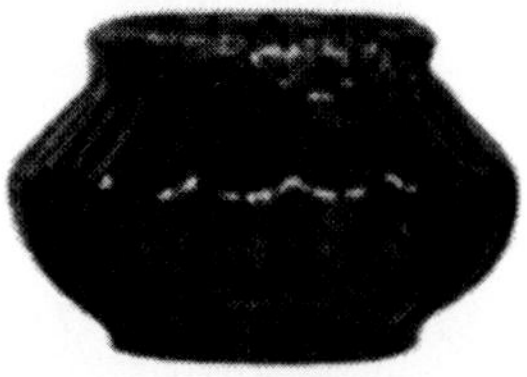

No. 178
8 in., $36.00

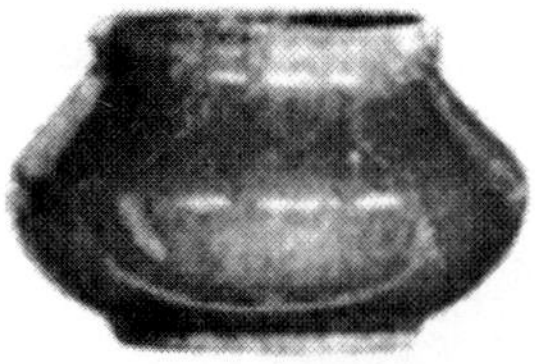

No. 179
8 in., $36.00

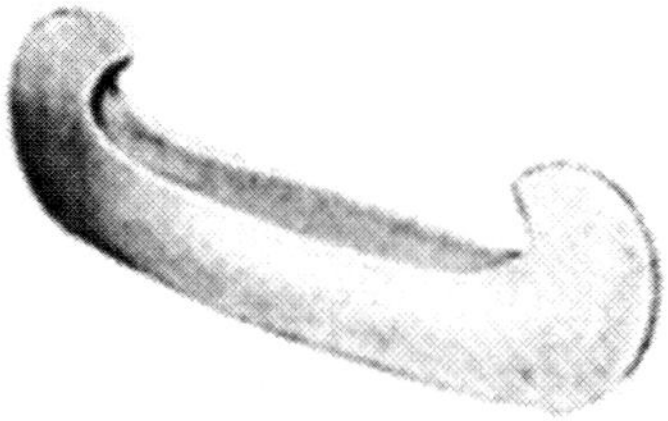

No. 253
11½ in., $24.00

No. 181
7½ in., $36.00

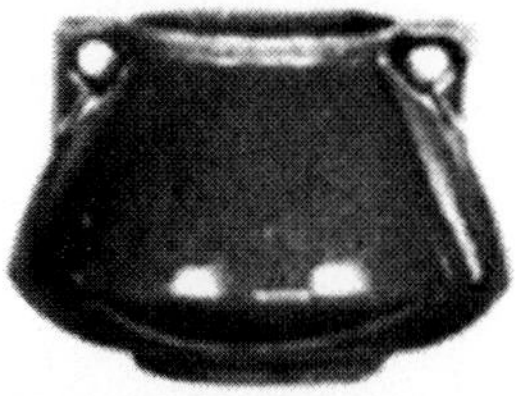

No. 182
8 in., $36.00

No. 143
7 in., $30.00

Muncie Clay Products Co., Muncie, Indiana

ARTISTIC POTTERY

No. 250 — $18.00
$3.00 per pair

No. 254 — $18.00
$3.00 per pair

No. 252
10 in., $24.00

No. 251
9 in., $18.00

No. 141
9 in., $24.00

No. 200
6 in., $18.00
3½ in., $12.00

No. 255
4 in., $3.60

No. 257
$18.00
$3.00 per pair

No. 148
9 in., $18.00

No. 172
8 in., $18.00

No. 268
Tobacco Jar
$30.00

No. 271
Candy Jar
$30.00

Muncie Clay Products Co., Muncie, Indiana

MUNCIE POTTERY CATALOG NO. 29/
MUNCIE CLAY PRODUCTS CATALOG 1929

MUNCIE POTTERY

Catalog No. 29

MUNCIE CLAY PRODUCTS CO.
Muncie Pottery
MUNCIE, INDIANA

Catalog and Price List

1929

Muncie Clay Products Co.
Muncie Potteries
MUNCIE, INDIANA

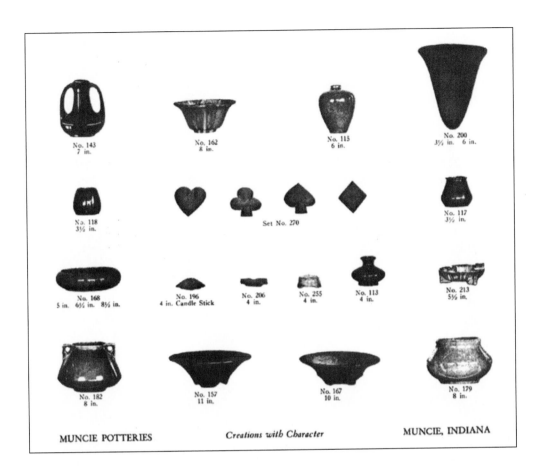

No. 143
7 in.

No. 162
8 in.

No. 115
6 in.

No. 200
3½ in.   6 in.

No. 118
3½ in.

Set No. 270

No. 117
3½ in.

No. 168
5 in.   6½ in.   8½ in.

No. 196
4 in. Candle Stick

No. 206
4 in.

No. 255
4 in.

No. 113
4 in.

No. 213
5½ in.

No. 182
8 in.

No. 157
11 in.

No. 167
10 in.

No. 179
8 in.

MUNCIE POTTERIES   *Creations with Character*   MUNCIE, INDIANA

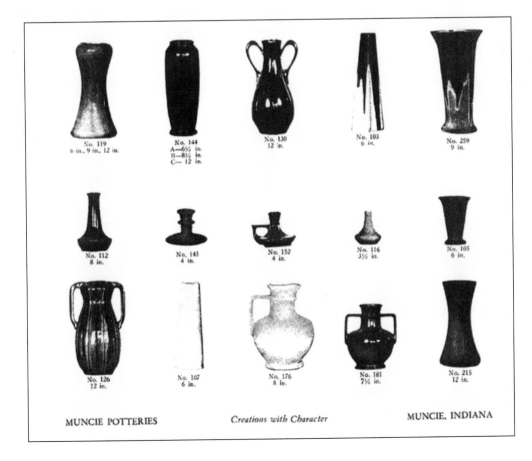

No. 119
6 in., 9 in., 12 in.

No. 144
A—6½ in.
B—8½ in.
C— 12 in.

No. 130
12 in.

No. 103
6 in.

No. 259
9 in.

No. 112
8 in.

No. 145
4 in.

No. 152
4 in.

No. 116
3½ in.

No. 105
6 in.

No. 126
12 in.

No. 107
6 in.

No. 176
8 in.

No. 181
7½ in.

No. 215
12 in.

MUNCIE POTTERIES   *Creations with Character*   MUNCIE, INDIANA

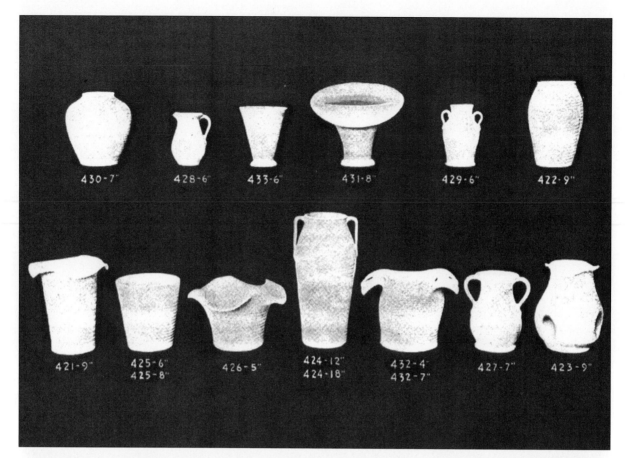

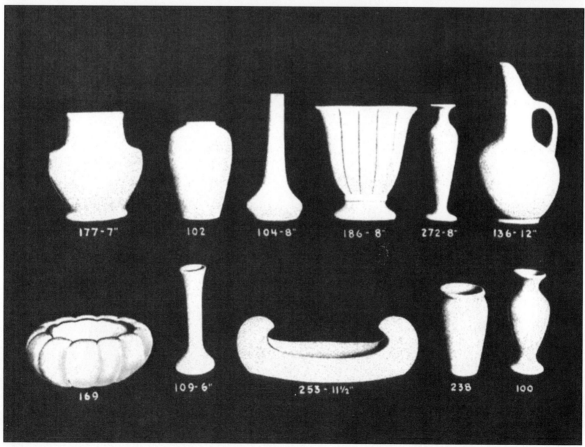

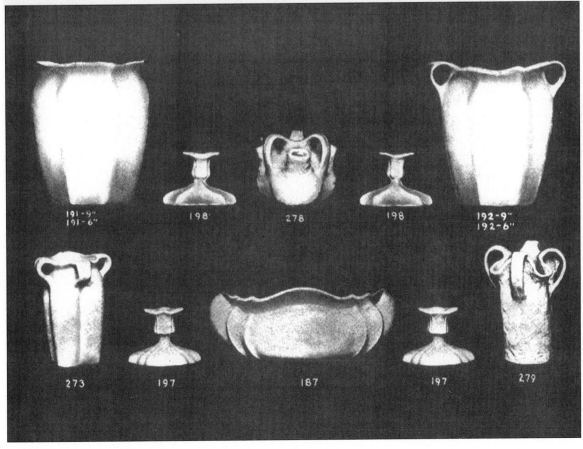

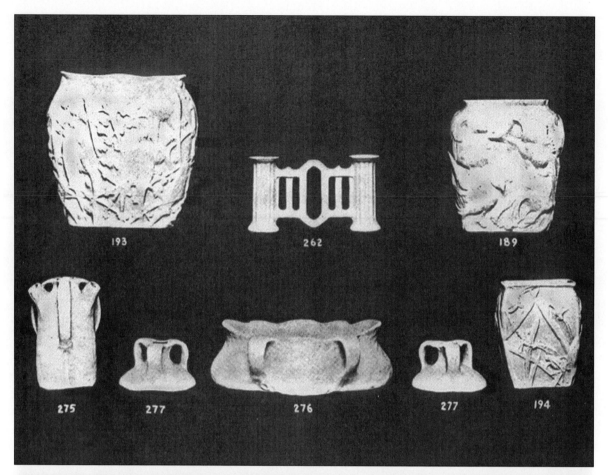

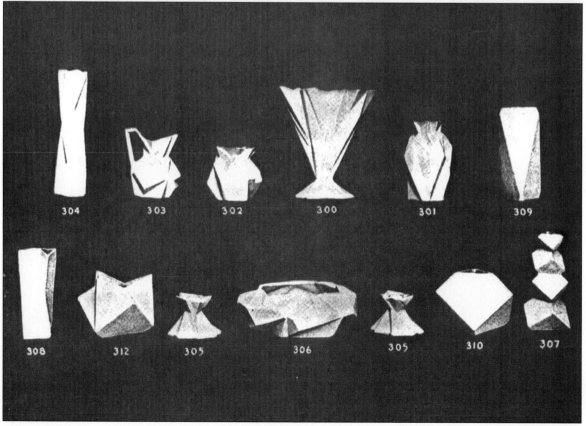

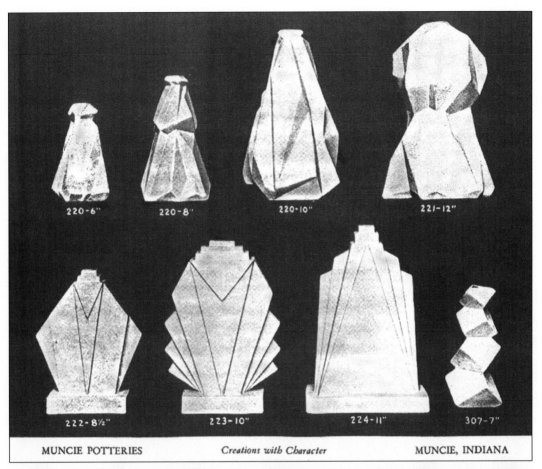

220-6"　220-8"　220-10"　221-12"

222-8½"　223-10"　224-11"　307-7"

MUNCIE POTTERIES　　*Creations with Character*　　MUNCIE, INDIANA

400-9"　402-6"　403-4"　404-6"　405-5"　406-12"

407-12"　401-13"　408-9"　409-13"

450-13"   451 - 8½"   455-10"   452 - 6½"   456 - 12"

457-10"   453-11"   458-8½"   454-10"   459 -12"

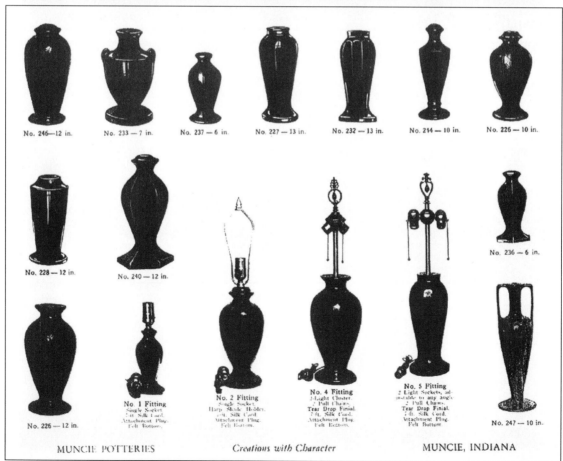

No. 246—12 in.   No. 233 — 7 in.   No. 237 — 6 in.   No. 227 — 13 in.   No. 232 — 13 in.   No. 214 — 10 in.   No. 226 — 10 in.

No. 228 — 12 in.   No. 240 — 12 in.   No. 236 — 6 in.

No. 226 — 12 in.

No. 1 Fitting
Single Socket.
2 ft. Silk Cord.
Attachment Plug.
Felt Bottom.

No. 2 Fitting
Single Socket.
Harp Shade Holder.
6 ft. Silk Cord.
Attachment Plug.
Felt Bottom.

No. 4 Fitting
3-Light Cluster.
3 Pull Chains.
Tear Drop Finial.
9 ft. Silk Cord.
Attachment Plug.
Felt Bottom.

No. 5 Fitting
2 Light Sockets, adjustable to any angle.
2 Pull Chains.
Tear Drop Finial.
9 ft. Silk Cord.
Attachment Plug.
Felt Bottom.

No. 247 — 10 in.

MUNCIE POTTERIES   *Creations with Character*   **MUNCIE, INDIANA**

BIBLIOGRAPHY

INTERVIEWS

1994   Ray Jones, Gill Clay Pot Company employee
1995   Richard and William Sacksteder, sons of Aladdin Mfg. founders
1995   Gerald and Pat Hahn, Muncie Pottery collectors
1995   Casey Tucker, Muncie Pottery collector
1996   Francis Burton, Benham family employee
1997   Fred Wilkins, grandson of James Wilkins
1998   Kenny West , Gill Clay Pot Company employee
1998   Ed Arnold, Pittsville Pottery collector
1998   Nicol Knappen, past president, Wisconsin Pottery Assoc.

BOOKS

Delaware Co. Index of Names and Firms: 1939 W.P.A. project
History of Delaware County. Edited by Frank D. Haimbaugh. Indianapolis: Historical Publishing Co., 1924.
L & W Books Better Electric Lamps of the 20s and 30s. Gas City, Indiana: L&W Books, 1997.
The Art Of Pot Making, Journal of the American Ceramics Society, Vol. 3, No. 8, Aug. 20, 1920: Chas. O. Grafton.
Gifford, David. *Collector Encyclopedia of Camark Pottery.* Paducah, Kentucky: Collector Books, 1997.
Kovel, Ralph and Terry. *American Art Pottery.* New York: Crown Publishing, 1993.
Henzke, Lucile. *Art Pottery of America.* Atglen, Pennsylvania: Schiffer Publishing.
Purviance, Evan and Louise. *Zanesville Art Tile.* Des Moines, Iowa: W. H. Books, 1972.
Whitlatch, George I. *The Clay Resources of Indiana.* Division of Geology, Indianapolis: W.B. Burford Printing Co., 1933.
Wilson, Jack. *Phoenix & Consolidated Glass 1920–1980.* Marietta, Ohio: Antique Publications, 1989.
Wires, E. Stanley: Norris Schneider: Moses Mesre. *Zanesville Decorative Tiles.* Zanesville Ohio: published by Schneider, Mesre, 1972.

MUNCIE POTTERY NEWSPAPER ARTICLES

Anon. "Unusual attention is attracted by park at No. 2 factory of Gill Clay Pot Company." *Muncie Morning Star,* Sunday August 17, 1919.
Anon. "Local company's name changed." *Muncie Morning Star,* January, 27, 1931.
Anon. "Gill golden wedding." *Muncie Morning Star,* December 15, 1935.
Anon. "Illness fatal to prominent manufacturer." *Muncie Morning Star,* March 25, 1939.
Anon. "Glass melting pots made by hand." *Muncie Star,* August 1, 1948.
Anon. "Old picture recalls Armistice parade here in 1918." *Muncie Star,* November 11, 1949.
Anon. "James Wilkins retired potter dies in Nebraska." *Muncie Star,* August 27, 1950.
Anon. "John H. Gill hit by auto, fatally hurt." *Muncie Evening Press,* December 5, 1966.
Branigin, E. M.: "Clay products show growth." *Muncie Morning Star,* November 8, 1925.
Brewer, Don. "An introduction to Muncie Pottery." *The Antique Trader Weekly.* Dubuque, Iowa: June 19, 1985.
Chapman, Steve. "Empty building presents hazards." *Muncie Star,* May 6, 1968.
Loy, Bob. "Old Gill Clay plant is destroyed by fire." *Muncie Star,* October 26, 1968.
Scott, Kathleen. "Made in Muncie." *Muncie Star,* April 23, 1993.
Slabaugh, Seth. "It was a gas." *Muncie Star Press,* February 14, 1998.
Spurgeon, Bill. "Our neighborhood." *Muncie Star,* May 30, 1995.
———— . "Our neighborhood." *Muncie Star,* June 2, 1995.

ALADDIN NEWSPAPER ARTICLES

"Aladdin Trade Mark dispute ended." *Lighting and Lamps,* Dec. 1935
Anon. "Electrical plants will consolidate." *Muncie Star,* November 4, 1923.
Anon. "Lamp company grows rapidly." *Muncie Star,* November 29, 1925.
Anon. "Lamp company plans addition." *Muncie Star,* September 21, 1927.
Anon. "Household Electric Inc." *Muncie Star,* September 25, 1927.
Anon. "Retherford plant bought." *Muncie Star,* February 15, 1928.
Anon. "Airplane converted to sales room by Muncie firm." *Muncie Sunday Star,* April 27, 1930.
Anon. "Sacksteder selling plant at Elwood." *Muncie Evening Press,* December 11, 1957.
Anon. "Sacksteder family forms new corporation." *Muncie Star,* July 16, 1959.
Anon. "Hoosier artist, prize winner William Fager dead at 76." *Muncie Star,* November 1, 1973.
Heiss, Willard and Virginia. "Muncie Pottery made Aladdin Lamp bases." *Antique Week,* August 10, 1987.

BOYS TOWN NEWSPAPER ARTICLES

Anon. "Pottery interests visitors." *Boys Town Times,* December 12, 1941.
Anon. "William Wilkins, teacher, dies of heart ailment." *Boys Town Times,* October 8, 1954.
Boys Town Times, February 25, 1944.
Boys Town Times, May 9, 1947.
Boys Town Times, August 11, 1950.
Rans, Jon W. "English-born ceramist founded Boys Town Pottery." *Antique Week,* Knightstown, Indiana: Mayhill Publications, May 19, 1997.

PITTSVILLE POTTERY NEWSPAPER ARTICLES

Anon. "To the parish priest of Pittsville and the pottery plant's president." *Milwaukee Journal,* September 17, 1939.
Knappen, Nicol. "Pottery lives on for collectors." *Antique Trader Weekly,* September 1997.

CATALOG REPRINTS

1933 Aladdin Lamps available from J. W. Courter, 3935 Kelly Road, Kevil, Kentucky. 42053-9431.

PERSONAL CORRESPONDENCE

April 24, 1908 from Gill Clay Pot Co. to all customers.
October 5, 1911 from Gill Clay Pot Co. to A.G. Matthews
November 10, 1911 from Harry Gill to Gill Clay Pot Co.
July 17, 1921 from Harry Gill to Charles Gill.
1924 draft biography from Charles Grafton.
September 23, 1924 from C. V. Grafton to Iva M. Webster.
November 12, 1964 from John H. Gill to Julian Harrison Toulouse.
September 4, 1968 from Mearl Keppler to Ellen Donahue.
October 4, 1973 from Charles Sherrell to Lucile Henzke.
June 6, 1982 from Gertrude Snyder to Don Brewer.
Sept. 27, 1995 from Dick Sacksteder to Jon Rans.
March 4, 1996 from David Gifford to Jon Rans.
April 16, 1996 Wisconsin Pottery Association release by Dave Knutzen, Betty Knutzen, and Jeffery Grayson.

PHOTO CREDITS

Swift Photograph Collection, Ball State University, Muncie, Indiana.
Page 20, Ruth Chin Photography, Muncie, Indiana.
Page 21, reprinted by permission, copyright 1968 *Muncie Star.*
Mike Borg, Boys Town color photographs.
Brent Holloway, factory photographs.

239

Schroeder's
ANTIQUES
Price Guide

. . . is the #1 best-selling antiques & collectibles value guide on the market today, and here's why . . .

Identification & Values of Over 50,000 Antiques & Collectibles

8½ x 11, 612 Pages, $12.95

• *More than 450 advisors, well-known dealers, and top-notch collectors work together with our editors to bring you accurate information regarding pricing and identification.*

• *More than 45,000 items in almost 550 categories are listed along with hundreds of sharp original photos that illustrate not only the rare and unusual, but the common, popular collectibles as well.*

• *Each large close-up shot shows important details clearly. Every subject is represented with histories and background information, a feature not found in any of our competitors' publications.*

• *Our editors keep abreast of newly developing trends, often adding several new categories a year as the need arises.*

If it merits the interest of today's collector, you'll find it in *Schroeder's*. And you can feel confident that the information we publish is up to date and accurate. Our advisors thoroughly check each category to spot inconsistencies, listings that may not be entirely reflective of market dealings, and lines too vague to be of merit. Only the best of the lot remains for publication.

Without doubt, you'll find
SCHROEDER'S ANTIQUES PRICE GUIDE
the only one to buy for
reliable information and values.

COLLECTOR BOOKS
A Division of Schroeder Publishing Co., Inc.